A Sprig of White Heather and a Scottish Lass

A Sprig of White Heather and a Scottish Lass

Anne Angelo

Library of Congress Control Number: 2022908472
ISBN: Hardcover   978-1-6698-8838-3
                 Softcover   978-1-6698-8837-6
                 eBook   978-1-6698-8836-9

Print information available on the last page.

Rev. date: 05/12/2022

To order additional copies of this book, contact:
Xlibris
AU TFN: 1 800 844 927 (Toll Free inside Australia)
AU Local: (02) 8310 8187 (+61 2 8310 8187 from outside Australia)
www.Xlibris.com.au
Orders@Xlibris.com.au
838782

NOTE FROM THE AUTHOR

THIS IS BASED on my story, the life of Anne Angelo. My childhood was full of hardships; both the climate and my father were very severe. At a very early age, I learned to fend for myself—from learning to drive a bus, to helping my brother sell whisky to the sailors in port.

When I finished high school, I was apprenticed to a chemist. After I had completed my time, Father prevented me from sitting for the examinations to qualify. How he tried to marry me off! I applied for the position of governess with a family in France and was fortunate to gain it. I was virtually taken into the family, and for three years we were inseparable. However, the effects of the depression finally forced my employer to reduce his expenses, and the grand house had to be closed.

I tried hard to obtain other employment but did not succeed. As things turned out, this was very lucky for me, for I found myself put in charge of running the house as a private hotel.

Two years later, Europe was on the brink of war. I decided I had to visit Invergordon to see my mother, and it was there that I found myself before that fateful day of 1 September 1939, when the unthinkable happened. War was declared!

To be continued.

CONTENTS

1. Reflections 1
2. Early Childhood 15
3. Formative Years 22
4. Father's Cars 32
5. Mr Ross Is Killed..41
6. The Scholarship 47
7. The Fleet...56
8. Apprentice With The Chemist 66
9. The Position Vacant 75
10. France..80
11. My New Home...91
12. Settling In 100
13. The House 107
14. Relations...114
15. Switzerland 121
16. St Malo..136
17. Monte Carlo 144
18. The Depression Hits 151
19. Algeria...162
20. Return To Lille...170
21. The Threat Approaches 176

CHAPTER 1

Reflections

WAITING IS NEVER easy. For women in wartime—waiting for word of their men—waiting becomes a soul-destroying purgatory. Day crawls into night, and night drags on into yet another dreary day. The months slip past with nothing to show for them. It's like sitting alone in a slow train being carried through an interminable succession of tunnels not knowing where you're going. Or if you're really going anywhere.

Is it all in vain? Is he dead? Was he blown to bits and nobody knows? Or maybe they've caught him. Is he a poor broken ghost shuffling round in some frightful concentration camp, so broken he wants you to never see him again? After months of waiting, every possible doubt comes to torment you. Doesn't he think you're still waiting? Has he found some new love and forgotten you? Did he never really mean all those lovely things you planned together? Are you letting your life drift away into emptiness for nothing?

These and a thousand other doubts come and gnaw at you. They press closer and speak louder as the time drifts away. And there are no answers. All you can do is cling to the shreds of your faith—and trust—and hope.

Our parting had been a frantic few moments clouded by fear and haste. He had said, 'You have to get out. Go back to Scotland. You should be safe enough there, and I'll know where to find you. When I can, I'll be in touch.'

I'd got away safely, but I had no way of knowing if he had. He'd have been a much greater prize. I was pretty sure he was in military intelligence although he'd never said so. It was the only thing that could explain his odd comings and goings.

He'd been a major when we'd first met in the early days of the war.

If he hadn't got away, he'd certainly have been questioned, and they'd have shot what was left.

I couldn't write anywhere to find out if he was safe. I didn't know his full name. I'd asked him often enough, but he'd never told me. All I had was his Christian name—Gerald. At first, during those days of the phoney war, curiosity had made me go round asking anyone I could, trying to find out. I'd had French and British Army officers billeted with me in the hotel I had in Lille in the north of France. I'd asked them, but I'd had to stop it. I'd been cautioned by no less a person than HRH the Duke of Gloucester, who'd come to a conference.

'You just stop it, young miss,' he'd said after he'd satisfied himself as to my identity. 'If he didn't tell you his name, you can be jolly sure he had good reason not to. We're not over here for a picnic, you know. This is war. And remember, what you don't know, you can't be made to tell. Do I make myself clear?'

He had. He'd made himself so clear that I never asked again. And his words about 'can't be made to tell' made a lot of things clear when the Germans came.

So I had no way of knowing if he was alive or dead. And I had no way of finding out. I could only stay and wait for a message.

But my father's house wasn't my home. It hadn't been since he made me live when I was twenty. I'd made a home for myself in my hotel in Lille. Life in Invergordon had been impossible because of his treatment of me and my brother Peter and our mother. Father's hatred of us all had ruled everything in our lives. It was a hatred that had been born on the very day of their wedding.

When he married my mother, he'd thought he was going to be the heir to her family's large estates in the South of France. They'd had no male offspring of their own, and he thought that by marrying the eldest daughter, he would naturally inherit. But he'd showed his hand too soon, and they'd disowned their daughter and cut her off. Father had been left with a bride he'd never loved or even really wanted. In his eyes, he had been cheated. Instead of becoming a wealthy landowner, he got an extra mouth to feed. And as I and then Peter came along, his hatred had carried over onto us. We were more mouths to be fed. Mouths he'd never wanted.

And for me, there was something else. He thought it was his right to find a husband for me. It had been the custom in the part of Italy his father had been reared in. And this, coupled with his desire for revenge, had caused him to make all sorts of nice little plans for me. If he'd seen a chance of blocking things between Gerald and me, he'd have delighted in it. And there'd been a fair chance that he had.

In his grandparents' part of Italy, the fathers arranged who their children would marry. A suitable boy and girl would be matched up and a date set. The wishes of the young couple didn't come into it. If there were any objections, the pair would be locked in a bedroom for the night. Whatever the events of the night were, they usually married afterwards. Because no one else would have them. He hadn't gone as far as that with me, but I never knew what he would try. I'd had a couple of experiences.

When I was thirteen—I admit I was a well-developed thirteen—he'd thought his foreman would be good for me. Only my own quick wits and stout knee had saved me. Father had been furious. 'You didn't have to do that to him,' he stormed. 'He's a good man, and I'm payin' him top money. I'd have seen he married you. We'd have kept the money in the family.' It didn't matter that Toshack had a face like a spawning salmon and was utterly repulsive.

The next try came when I was eighteen. There'd probably been many others planned that had fallen through. The idea was close to his heart. This time it was the village constable. No doubt he thought that Geordie, being big and the law, would fix me. But he thought it necessary to warn him: 'Ye'll maybe find you have your hands full. She's a bit of a tiger.' Geordie told me himself. He also told me, 'We canna get married, sweetie, ye ken.' He was broad Scots. 'It's me mither, d'ye see? She'll no' let me. She says ye're no' guid enough for me. But I dinna doubt, when we've had a bairn or two, she'll change her mind. Och sweetie, we'll have fine bairns, you and me.' He thought he was offering me the world.

Some of the girls I'd been at school with had been trapped with that sort of thing and found themselves deserted after a couple of little ones had arrived. The fathers had started again elsewhere. Geordie didn't give up easily. For months he used to come and serenade under my window when the moon was full. Mother and I had many a quiet laugh at him out there.

Father was well known even then. He was the only man in the entire Highlands who could make precision parts for any kind of motor car or engine. In those days, they all had to be made by hand and Joe Angelo's Mechanical and Engineering Works had a name for reliability. He also got most of the work on the engines of the warships at the naval base. He had fifteen men working for him. As an extra moneymaker, he hired out cars and motorbikes to the Navy men. Or rather, Peter and I had to earn our keep. The garage and works were at the end of the garden.

So maybe by eighteen, I had become 'a bit of a tiger.' But if I had, it was entirely due to him and his treatment of me, of Peter, and of our mother. He gave us hell. Peter and I got what pocket money we had by selling flowers and then whisky to the sailors. When I was eleven, I had to drive the great lumbering bus taking people to the sporting fixtures at sixpence a head. I had to have a two-gallon benzene tin behind me on the seat to keep me forward far enough to reach the controls. Mother had to grow the potatoes, which, with the porridge and salt herrings, was our food.

Some people think we ourselves are responsible for what we become. But it's not so. What we are is almost completely due to things beyond our control. We make some decisions, yes, of course. But they're only relatively small ones. And even they are made in light of what's happened to us in the past.

Shakespeare makes Cassius say in *Julius Caesar*, 'The fault, dear Brutus, is not in our stars but in ourselves that we are underlings.' But he is wrong. What we are is basically in our stars and not in ourselves.

ANNE ANGELO

'Stars' has nothing to do with horology. It plans the circumstances and environment into which we are born.

Primarily, we are the result of the genes we inherit from our parents. After we're born, the lives those parents have lived have their effects on us. We are further shaped by the place where we live, the climate, and what happens to us in our formative years. Everybody we meet has an influence on us, either for good or bad, just as we have an influence on them. A wheelbarrow or a motorcar inevitably bears signs of how it's been treated. Whether it's been looked after and cared for. Or whether it's been roughly used and neglected and left out in the weather. Humans are even more so: the effects can't be avoided.

I was back in my father's house not because in any way I wanted to be. I was back because in my Gerald's eyes, and I knew he really cared for me, it was the safest place for me to be.

The security for the naval base was also protection. And it was the only place where I could stay indefinitely until he could contact me.

I'd never told him what things were really like and what my father had in mind for me. You don't tell things like that when you want people to like and respect you. Our last moments had been frantic. There'd been no time for explanations or arguments. He'd been risking his life. I simply had to go and do as he said.

To have done anything else, to have gone anywhere else would have been throwing away everything I held most dear. He would never have known where I'd gone, and I wouldn't have been able to let him know. I'd never known where I could get in touch with him. I'd tried my best to let him know where I was. Yes, I had. I'd written articles in the papers hoping he'd see them and know I'd got home all right.

I missed Peter. He and I had been more like two brothers than brother and sister. I'd have felt better if he'd been around. But he'd gone off in the Navy. The last I heard, he'd been in Edinburgh, but he could have gone anywhere—on a ship—or even sunk.

Our house was on Ross Street. Ross Street runs nearly due east and west from the High Street down to where Hugh Miller Street and the Shore Road meet at the Navy Yards. Invergordon was an important naval base in World War I. If you stood on the corner of the High Street and looked along Ross Street, you would be looking out over where the Navy Yards used to be, out over Cromarty Firth and Moray Firth to the North Sea.

It was out there that the gales and hurricanes and blizzards brewed up to come raging in on us, as if determined to drive us all out of the place. The sea went berserk, rising up in huge green mountains to tear ships from their moorings and come rushing on to smash against the sea wall. Blocked there, great sheets of spume were flung up for the wind to grab and hurl at us. The house trembled. Frozen droplets were fired against our upper windows. The big pear tree at the rear turned its back and shielded its face in its arms.

The house still stands end on to the street and thus broadside to the full force. Where Hugh Miller and the Shore Road and Ross Street meet, it made a kind of funnel that directed everything at us. Many were the nights I pulled the covers over my head and waited for the house to be blown over and bowled along the street.

We had no protection to windward. There was room for three or four houses there, but we had it all for our garden. At the end, there were the two small sheds where we kept the oats for our porridge and the salt herrings, but they were too small to break the wind. And the garage and works buildings beyond were too far away.

After the size and sumptuous splendour of my hotel, it was no wonder that I found the waiting tedious. There, there'd always been something going on. There'd been every luxury the human brain could devise. Even when the Germans came, there'd been plenty to do. One had the feeling one was doing something useful. Life had a spice to it.

Here, I was doing nothing.

I was twenty-nine. I knew that if I were going to have all the things women naturally want, I didn't have much more time for sitting around. But against that, I knew I could never find contentment with any other man. There'd never be anybody else for me. I'd resolved—at least until some better idea for finding him came along—to wait here until the war was over. It seemed as if we were going to win. And then go back to Lille to my hotel again. I thought that was the best place for him to come looking for me, and there, at any rate, I'd be picking up the threads and getting on with my life.

Ever since we parted, I'd had a worry. Had he tried to contact me in those months I'd been getting home? I thought it likely he had. He'd have wanted to make sure I was safe. And if he had, what had he been told? Father hadn't known where I was. He hadn't even known I was on the way home, but he was smart enough to have caught on. He'd love to have put a spoke in our wheel. And if he had, what had he told him? It was in my mind the whole time.

I'd been home a couple of weeks when I got the perfect way to settle it. The *Dundee Weekly News* approached me to write some articles on my experiences in France under the Nazi heel. It was the ideal way of letting people know I was home and safe and sound. I did a series from 20 September to 25 October. They gave me front-page rating, with my name and photo bold and clear. There could be no mistake who it was and where I was. I garbled them as much as I could to protect the people still over there. I hoped some of them might be seen in France. Or at least talked about.

But as I said in the beginning, waiting isn't easy. For women like me, in wartime—waiting for word of their men—waiting becomes a soul-destroying purgatory. Days crawl into nights and nights drag on into yet another dreary day. It's like sitting alone in a slow train being taken through an interminable succession of tunnels, not knowing what's going to be at the end.

In the time I'd been home, I'd hardly set foot out of the house. It certainly wasn't easy. I was in the parlour reading *Hamlet*. It had rained all night, and I had a good fire on. I'd just read the tragic duel scene and was thinking about it and feeling sorry for poor Hamlet. It seemed to me we had lots in common. He'd never had the chance of a proper life either. He'd had the intrigues of his uncle. I'd had my father, and now the war. My thoughts were broken by Mother coming in. It surprised me; she seldom did.

'I hope I'm not wrong, dear,' she said, putting her hands on my shoulders from behind. 'But I think your man's here. There's an army officer at the door asking for you. Will you go, or shall I bring him in here?'

'There's a what? Oh, there's not, is there? Oh heavens! No, it's all right. I'll go.' And after a quick dab at my hair in the sideboard mirror, I went.

But as soon as I saw him there, framed against the light, it all went cold. It wasn't him. He wasn't tall enough, and he wasn't big enough. My Gerald's a good six feet two and big with it. This fellow was no bigger than I was. He was a major. He had a briefcase in his hand.

'Yes, Major. Do you want to see me?'

'Miss Angelo? Miss Anne Angelo?' He was about with a small moustache.

'Yes.' I wondered what on earth he could want with me. I hadn't had very good experiences with army officers—except with my Gerald, of course, but he's one in a million—and with majors especially. I'd found that British, French, or German—they all had scant regard for the rights and welfare of civilians.

'Major J. H. Hughes, from the War Office, London." He took an identity card from his top left pocket, opened it, and held it for me to see. "Could you spare me a few minutes? I'd like to have a talk with you.'

'Yes, Major. Go ahead. What's it about?'

'Well, er, would it be all right if I came in? It's not very convenient here, and it is perishing cold.'

I realised it was cold. His words floated away in little white puffs.

I didn't want to let him in. I couldn't think of any business he could have with me. But he'd said he'd come up from London to see me, so there had to be something.

'All right, Major. Come in.' And I stood aside to let him. 'Go straight ahead. The first door on the left there.'

I was closing the door when suddenly it came to me that it must be Gerald. That's what he'd come about. Something must have happened. I felt cold dread as I went in.

But he'd put his cap and briefcase on the table and was standing with his back to the fire and with my Shakespeare open in his hand.

ANNE ANGELO

It jarred on me. It didn't fit. I hadn't let him in to read my Shakespeare. He had no right to touch it. His words made it worse.

'*Hamlet* eh? Great stuff. Know it well myself. Marvellous fellow, old Shakespeare. All the finer philosophies of life, what? Good reading, every word of it.'

'Oh, you think so, do you?' I took it from him and turned to Julius Caesar and the place where it says something about the fault not being in our stars but in ourselves. And I read it to him.

'That's just rubbish, Major. Hamlet wasn't a prince because of anything he'd done. It wasn't his fault his uncle did what he did. And he couldn't help his mother being like she was. Nor was Ophelia's death his fault. It was all in his stars. He had to do what he had to do. But that's enough of that. Suppose you get on with it. Tell me what you've come for. If you've got bad news for me, let me have it. I've had bad news before.'

I knew it was wrong as soon as I'd said it. He was so taken aback.

'I'm very sorry,' he said, 'if I've offended you. I certainly didn't intend to. And you're wrong about me having bad news for you. I haven't. I don't know why you should think I have. I've come up here because we think you might be able to help us.'

He took his briefcase from the table and went across to the settee under the window.

'Is it all right if I sit here?' he said, sitting there as he said it. It was done so casually that I didn't see the reason for it then. From his case he took a file which he opened on his knee and studied.

'Yes,' he said after a minute or two. 'Well, there's just a couple of questions first, if you don't mind. But I think you'll see why.'

I took a chair from the table and turned it so I could sit with my arms on its back, facing him.

'Well, what are they?'

'Have you ever been to Europe?'

It was so silly it made me suspicious. Surely they must have seen at least some of my articles down in London. I realised why he'd sat where he had. His face was in shadow while mine was in the light. The Germans and the French had used the same trick.

'Could I see that identity card again, please, Major?'

This time I took it. The photo was unmistakably him. And the rest seemed authentic enough. But so did the ones that I'd personally faked. The uniform looked genuine, but that didn't mean anything either. Our men had worn genuine German uniforms. I gave it back to him and resolved to go carefully.

'Yes, I have.'

'Could you tell me what parts exactly?'

'Yes. I was in France, Monaco, and Switzerland. Italy, Algeria, and Spain.'

'Good. We're interested in France. What parts of it do you know?'

'Well, I've been to most of it. Pretty. Well, from Dunkirk to Marseille. I spent many holidays along the centre coast.'

'Ah yes. That's what we're interested in. The centre coast. What areas do you know?'

'Oh, St Lunaire, St Nazaire, St Malo, Avranches, Bayeux, and Le Fecamp. I know them fairly well. Is that enough?'

'Yes, indeed. Very good. And you said you were on holidays. How did you travel? By train or car?'

'Always by car. I had good ones, and I like driving.'

'Then you'd know the roads, wouldn't you? And how did you find the French standards of driving? Have any accidents?'

'Yes, as a matter of fact, I did. I had two. But they weren't with the French. They were both with members of your own army. One was with a dispatch-rider and caused me no end of bother. But the other was the happiest thing that ever happened to me. Through it I met the most wonderful man in the world. But it was his driver's fault, not mine.'

'I see.' And I thought there was a smile in his eyes. 'And I think you said you were based in Paris. Is that right?'

'No, it's not. I didn't say anything of the kind. I was based in Lille. But what's this all about, Major? I think I've been patient enough.'

'Yes, you have. But there is just one more. What do you know about white heather? Does it grow anywhere else but in Scotland?'

That did it. Like the sun bursting through the clouds, it made everything clear. He was OK. He was only checking me. But the mention of white heather sent a great surge of joy through me. It proved at least that Gerald had known I was over there. So he must've been alive. And he probably still was. His hand could've written these questions. My face must have shown my feelings, for he came over and shook my hand warmly.

'I'm very pleased to meet you, Miss Angelo. Very pleased, indeed. You've had quite some experiences, haven't you?'

'But tell me, what have you really come up here to see me about?'

'Yes. Well, I suppose that's a fair question. But as I said in the first place, we think you might be able to help us. And now that I've spoken to you, I'm pretty sure you can. But I had to make sure of you before letting you know what it was.'

The clock on the sideboard broke in with its musical chimes of twelve.

'By Jove, is it really that?' he asked, looking at his watch. 'So it is. Oh good heavens! My poor driver! He must be frozen stiff out there. I say, would it be all right if he came in? Maybe he could wait in the kitchen or somewhere. We're going to be a while yet. And do you think there'd be any chance of a cup of tea? We had to get away early, and it was a long drive.'

He went out and got his driver, and I took him into the kitchen and left him with Mother.

*   *   *

"Another cup, Major?" I asked as he drained his cup and set it down.

'No, thanks. I've done fine, thank you very much. And do tell your mother her cake was much appreciated. So you don't think it's a good idea for you to go back to France?'

'No, I don't. Not for me. I'm too well known. I was plain lucky with that last thing. To go back again would be asking for trouble. No, there must be others better than me.'

'Yes, but you know the whole area so well. And we'd look after you. You'd have an entirely new identity. We'd air-drop you in, and you'd have all the assistance you need. I think you'd be able to do a lot.'

'I don't think so. I don't think I'd be any good to you at all. They'd simply watch everywhere I went, note all my contacts, and then move in and clean up the lot."

'Yes, all right, if that's the way you feel. And by the way, those articles you wrote were seen in Germany. They caused quite a stir. Anyway, thanks for all this.' He tapped the file he was holding. 'It's just what we're looking for.'

'Is there any real chance of making a landing? In the face of what they've got massed along those beaches?'

'I'm afraid I can't discuss that with you. But tell me, what happened at Fecamp? They got you off all right, didn't they? But you didn't turn up on the other side. What happened?'

'Oh yes. They got me off all right. Everything was going fine. But some English and German motor-torpedo-boats started having a go at each other right ahead of us by the English coast. We had to turn back. They put me ashore again in France. I had to get back to Lille and then go right through France to Marseille and then to Spain. I got to Gibraltar and came home on a coal-boat.'

'Oh, so that's where you got to. And how long did that take you?'

'A couple of months. I got here in September. That was 1941. I did the articles about a fortnight later.'

He opened the file, turned a couple of pages and made some notes.

'Yes. Well, I think that tidies everything up.' And he closed it. Would you mind getting my driver for me, please?' He put the file into his briefcase and picked up his cap.

'Oh, but just a moment. I have something for you. You have to sign for it.' From a side pocket he took a small packet wrapped in brown paper and gave it to me. It had a typewritten note attached 'To be handed to Miss Angelo—*personally*. In no circumstance to any other person. Obtain her signature.'

As soon as I took it, I knew what it was. I flexed it in my hand to make sure. There was no doubt about it. It was Mother's soft-backed copy of Robbie Burns's poems which I'd given to Gerald. He'd asked me for it. He'd said he'd always carry it in his top left pocket. 'You never know, it might turn a bullet,' he'd said. I'd known what he meant and loved him for it. Now he'd sent it back like this.

'Where did you get this, Major?'

'It was with the file, Miss. Why? Is there anything wrong?'

'Was there any message with it? Did you have to tell me anything?'

'No, Miss. Just what it says there. To get your signature.'

His face told me nothing. He was army again. I signed his receipt and gave it to him.

'You'll find your driver in the kitchen, straight across the hall. My mother will let you out. Good day to you, Major.' And I left him there and went up to my room. From my window, I watched them go out, carefully shut the gate, and drive away.

They were so typically army. They'd come,- for their own purposes; having got what they'd wanted, they'd gone. There'd never be a thought for me. But they'd broken the one link I'd had. They'd put an emptiness where I'd had a small warmth of satisfaction. And they'd left me more doubts. Doubts I couldn't find answers for.

Why could he have sent it back? And why in that way? Why no explanation? If I'd done something, or if Father had said something about me, didn't I have the right to be told? Could all the happy times we'd had, all the things we'd been through together, be forgotten so easily? I could find no answers.

Or did it mean he was dead? Had they found it in his effects and sent it to me? But if that was it, would they have wanted a receipt? I didn't think so. Nor would they have worried about it not being given to anyone else. They'd have simply sent it with a covering letter and been done with it.

Those things suggested his hand. And that meant he was still alive. But I couldn't be sure. I was even less sure than I'd been before.

I tore the end of the wrapping away. It was my Burns, all right. The sprig of white heather Mother had put in it showed plainly between the ends of the pages. I tossed the thing into my drawer and closed it.

Far out to the east, where grey of sky met grey of sea, a faint gleam showed and vanished as Cromarty Light blinked its message out into the gathering gloom. At my window there, alone, I felt like that. I too was waiting for a ship that might, or might not, come. I wondered if I wouldn't be better off letting Father fix things for me. But I knew I could never do that. There was nothing for me to do but to wait.

*   *   *

ANNE ANGELO

CHAPTER 2

Early Childhood

I WAS ABOUT SIX when I first got frightened of my father. We thought he was going to kill us all. Mother took us upstairs so he couldn't. Her mother was dying. They lived in France, and her father wrote saying she had to go to her. But our father wouldn't let her. He made her have another baby instead. When her mother died, he took the letter to the University in Edinburgh. He went mad and smashed everything. I was always frightened of him after that.

A letter came from Bordeaux. It's a big city in the South of France where Mother's people lived. It was warm and sunny. Her father wrote it. He said her mother was dying and asking for her. She had to come quickly. I ran to the garage for Father. He was at work. It was morning, and Mother was making the bread.

I went out along Ross Street. I knew I wouldn't get through his den. It's always locked. He was in his office in the front by the benzene pump. He got cranky. I thought he would, that's why I only stood in the doorway. I was ready to run. He didn't like us going to the garage when the men were there. And he didn't like having to come home.

Father didn't like being home very much. He'd rather be in his den or go off somewhere. He always came home for his dinner, and mostly for his supper, but not always. Sometimes he just came and looked. If it was only salt herrings and potatoes, he sometimes went and got himself something in his den. He had all sorts of things in there. Lovely things. Things we never got. When he went to Inverness or Edinburgh to pick up a new car for a customer, he filled it up with fancy things. He got little barrels of grapes in sawdust and all sorts of salami sausages and cases of wines and whiskies. Sometimes when they had been playing cards late, he slept in there. And he had places in Dingwall and Beauly where he went and stayed. He had lady friends there. Dingwall is along the Cromarty Firth on the way to Inverness. Beauly is farther on, at the end of Beauly Firth. We always knew when he was going. He got all cleaned up and put on good clothes.

Mother read the letter to him. Father couldn't read French. He took the letter and envelope and looked at the stamp and the writing.

'Well?' he said. 'So what do you want me to do, eh? Sit down and cry? Is that what you want, eh? So she's dying. You think I care? After what they did? You think I forget our wedding and they kicked us out like the dogs? In front of everybody? Get out, he said. Get out of my house and never come back. You think I forget that? Now you think I cry 'cause his old woman is dying? Ha. I say it's good. Let her die.' He smoked his cigarette. When Father got cranky, it was easy to tell he was Italian stock.

'Don't be like that, Joe,' Mother said. 'That was seven years ago. That's all done and finished with. He wants us all to go. I think he wants to make amends. Oh, Joe, what a difference it will make if he does. It'll be better for all of us. We'll have to go. If you'll give me a hand, we can get away today. There's an awful lot to be done. And we'll need money. We might have to be away for a week or so. You can never tell. But oh, Joe! If only everything's going to be all right, at least!'

'What are you talking about? Go over there? You crazy. What for? Who wants to go over there, eh? You know how much it costs? You know how much it costs to go over there for one week? Where could I get that sort of money, eh? Come on, you tell me that. Where could I get that sort of money?'

Mother stopped working her dough and leaned on her hands while she looked at him.

'All right, Joe,' she said. 'If you really don't want to go, it doesn't matter. I'll go by myself. I'll have to. Father wouldn't have written like that, not after all this time, if it hadn't been serious. Just give me enough to get me there. Father will pay my way back.'

Father was going to smoke his cigarette again, but he stopped with it near his mouth. He tipped his head back so he could look at

ANNE ANGELO

Mother from under his cap. He did that when he was watching you and thinking. There was always trouble when he did it. His eyes got small and went right back into his head like little black coals. His mouth pulled in thin and nasty like it did when he was going to be cruel. Father always wore an old cloth cap. It was grubby with greasy black finger marks on it. He wore it even at table. He pulled the front down so you couldn't see his eyes. His pullover had greasy marks on it too. It was a roll neck one.

'So!' he said. 'So that's it, eh? Now we see what you are up to. It's the same old thing. Mamma, I wanna come home! I don't like it here. I don't wanna be married. Joe, he's cruel to me. I wanna come home, Mamma! Why don't you grow up, eh? What's the matter with you? You think I'm stupid or something?'

Mother didn't know what he was talking about. She just stared at him.

He shook the letter at her.

'This is your doing,' he said. He looked awfully cruel. 'You made him write this. You made him write so you could get back there, eh? You think I don't know? You only want the money one way, eh? And what happens then, eh? I tell you what happens. You don't come back. That's what happens. I know. It's all a trick. You don't come back, and I get stuck with these two. Hey, it's a big joke. Joe Angelo's woman makes him a big monkey. She gets him to give her the money, and she's run back to Mamma. Joe, he's left with the two kids. You think I'll let you do that, eh? Oh no! I'm stupid, all right, but not so stupid as that. You're going nowhere. You stay here.'

Mother told him to stop it. He was being silly. Of course she'd come back. She'd never said she wouldn't. But father wouldn't listen. He wanted to be nasty. He said she was no good. She wouldn't do the house. She couldn't cook, and she was too lazy to do the garden. He said the ground would freeze and we'd lose all the potatoes, and then he'd have to buy potatoes. His mother was never like this. She was always too busy. She had seven to look after and not so much money. He said that was Mother's trouble. She didn't have enough to do.

He told her to go upstairs to bed. She would have to have another baby. It would stop her from running home to her mother. He said if she wasn't in bed when he came up, he would tear all her things and she wouldn't get any money for new ones.

Mother was angry. She pulled the dough together and cleaned the bits off her fingers. She said he wouldn't dare. She would get the policeman. Father said it wouldn't be any good. He'd talked to the policeman, and the policeman had told him he could do as he liked.

Mother belonged to him. He was the boss, and he could do as he liked. No one could make any trouble. Father said if she didn't go upstairs quickly, he would tear all her things right there in the kitchen.

Mother's face went white. She was upset. She looked at me and then at Peter. We were round the side of the table. Peter was on tiptoes, pulling up on the edge of the table with both hands so he could see. Peter had black curly hair. Mother said it was just like Father's used to be. We were ready to run. Then she looked back at Father. He looked awful. Tears ran down her face. She took off her apron and folded it and put it over the dough. She put her head up straighter and touched her hair. Then she smoothed her dress and turned and went upstairs. Her face was sort of set as if she knew Father was going to be cruel.

He got out a bottle Of whisky and sat there drinking. When he put it away and went up, I took Peter, and we ran round to Geordie Ross's place. I went to school with Geordie. They lived at the back of us in King Street, but we had to go round along Outram Street because we couldn't climb the fence from our side.

We were lucky. It wasn't dole day, and Mrs Ross gave us dinner and let us stay. On dole day, you couldn't go near Geordie's place. His father came home raging drunk and lashed out at everybody. He hated us. He called us the forcigncrs.

It was dark when we got home. I lit a candle. I couldn't light the lamp. We didn't have electric lights in the house, only in the garage and in Father's den. I went up to see what was for supper, but the door was shut. I heard Mother crying. I heard her say, 'O Blessed Mother, why have you forsaken me? What have I done to deserve this?' So I didn't let on I was there. Their room was at the top of the stairs.

I had to get the supper and put Peter to bed. We had soup. There was

ANNE ANGELO

always a pot of soup at the back of our stove. It was big and round and shiny, with a long shiny handle. It was too heavy to move, so I had to get up on a chair to reach and dib some out. I slipped and I was lucky I was holding tight to the mantel shelf. Our stove was big and wide, and it went right back. It was awfully hot.

Father didn't come home. In the morning, I had to take a letter to the Post Office. It was going to France. We tried to get the potatoes dug, but it was too cold. Our mittens got wet as we were picking up the potatoes, and then they froze. Peter and I had to take the potatoes and put them in the pits in the shed. Mother wasn't very well. Trying to get the fork into the hard ground made her cry.

We thought she was crying because Father wouldn't let her go to France. I asked her, but she said it wasn't that. I asked her not to go away and leave us. We didn't have anybody else, and Father would be cruel to us. She said she didn't have anybody else either. She put down the fork and hugged us. She said she never wanted to leave us. She saw our mittens and boots were all wet and frozen, and she took us inside. She said if the potatoes froze, they froze. She didn't care.

We got them all in, though. We did a little bit every day so they were in before Father came home. But he still picked on her. He said she was lazy and she was making us hate him. He liked to see Mother cry. He was home only a few days, and then he went off to Edinburgh.

Mother thought there would be another letter, so we kept a lookout. But the postman didn't come. We saw him one morning along the street, and Mother went and asked him. He said there had been one. It was from France and it had black round the edges. He'd given it to Father. He wasn't allowed to bring letters to the house anymore. They all had to go to the garage. Father had been to the Post Office about it. Mother's face all puckered up, and she hurried home and went upstairs. She stayed there all day. She was awfully unhappy.

When Father came home a few days afterwards, she asked him for her letter. He was going upstairs to change. He had good clothes on, and he had his bag with him. He gave her the letter, but it had been opened.

Mother asked him who had opened it.

'I opened it,' he said. 'I want to know what's going on. I don't want any more tricks.'

Mother said that was silly because he couldn't read French.

Father said he'd taken it to a man at the University in Edinburgh, who had read it to him. It said her mother was dead and her father wasn't going to write again. He was going to give them Mont-de-Marsan, but because they hadn't gone to France, they weren't going to get it. They weren't going to get anything. It was all finished. Father got angry. He said her father was a cheat and no good. He was glad her mother was dead. He said he'd be glad when her father was dead too. He never ever wanted to hear of them again. He kept on until Mother was in tears.

She told him he was wicked to talk like that. The Good Lord would hear him, and he would be punished. She said Father had no right to open her letters and he had no right to let anybody else read them.

It made Father worse, and he started shouting. He said wicked things. She wasn't to talk to him and tell him what he could do. It was his house, and he was the boss. He said he would beat her up if she didn't keep quiet. He saw the dinner set on the dresser and swung his arm and fisted it all off onto the floor. He grabbed the small plates and things off the shelves and smashed them.

It was the good dinner set. It was their wedding present from my godmother, who was a real Countess. It was for thirty-two people. We'd never used it. Peter and I weren't allowed to touch it. She was the Countess of Vissochi. It's in Italy, near Monte Casino. She owned the whole village. It had her royal blue crest on it. He opened the dresser and took out the piles of big plates and smashed them onto the floor. Bits flew everywhere. He was frothing and shouting. He didn't know what he was doing. Mother got us behind her and out up the stairs. She put us under their bed, and then she went and got the potty. She stood by the door at the top of the stairs with it. I think she was going to hit him with it if he had come up. But he didn't. When he'd smashed it all, he stomped out and slammed the front door.

Mother came in and got us out, and we all sat on the bed. She hugged us and cried. She was shaking. After a while, she read her letter.

She said we were all in an awful mess, and she didn't know how it was going to end. She was sorry for Father. It was no wonder he got so mad. He had thrown away everything he'd ever wanted. She said it was all finished. We would all have to be as good as good because now he would hate us worse than ever, and there'd be nothing to hold him back.

The kitchen was in an awful mess. There was broken crockery everywhere. One bit had flown right to the back of the stove onto the lid of the soup pot. There was one cup handle still hanging from its hook. We left it there. Mother said it would remind Father how silly he had been. That dinner set would have fetched a lot of money. I was always scared of Father after that. You never knew what he would do.

*   *   *

CHAPTER 3

Formative Years

I WAS NEARLY NINE before I knew why Father was the way he was and what Mont-de-Marsan was. Mother only told us because she thought he was going to freeze to death in the blizzard. She thought it was the way her Good Lord was going to fix things for us. She prayed so we could all go to France where it was warm. She wanted us to get Mont-de-Marsan and have horses to ride and lots of fresh fruit.

It was the worst blizzard we'd ever had. Everything was snowed under for days. Rose was still in naps, but crawling. Mother had an awful time having her. Father picked at her the whole time. He was happy when she cried. He was like she'd said he'd be, like a cranky seagull having a peck and a screech at everybody. I got lots of porridge. He even had a go at Dr McKay.

Dr McKay was at our house often. He thought Mother was going to die. Father said she was only putting it on to make him sorry and spend his money. He didn't want Dr McKay to come at all. Dr McKay told him if he didn't stop it, he would put Mother into the hospital, and that would cost a lot more. Dr McKay liked us. When his car was in to get fixed, he came along and talked to us over the gate. He brought us things. Father nearly cried when he saw his bill for the baby. Dr McKay said having babies was nearly as dear as having motor cars. Father did all the work on Dr McKay's car.

When Father got cranky, he put me on porridge. It made me sick. He said there was nothing wrong with it. I would just have to get used to it. He watched to make sure that Mother doesn't try to give me anything else. Sometimes it was for days. I got so sick I couldn't go to school. He didn't believe in schools. He said they were a waste of time.

Children ought to work. He had to when he was small. He had to work hard. His people were awfully poor. They only had bare feet and rags. He said we ought to do the garden. We could go and wash parts in the garage. Kerosene wouldn't hurt our hands. Mother said we had to go to school. If we didn't, she would go to the Council about it.

The blizzard came when Father was away down in Edinburgh for another car. All the roads and the railway were blocked as far down as Manchester. Everything was shut down. There was no school. People were told to stay inside and keep warm. It came over the wireless. Father allowed us to have the wireless on for an hour every night. Mother was worried about him. He always went by train and drove back. If he was on his way home and got caught in it, he could be in trouble.

In the morning, it was still howling and shrieking and trying to get in. It was halfway up the windows. Mother put the wireless on to see if there was any news. It said people had frozen to death in their car down near Carlisle. We were having breakfast, and Mother suddenly stopped and crossed herself. She said that maybe it was the way the Good Lord was going to fix things for us. She said if it was, we would all be out of this place so quickly it wouldn't matter. She shut her eyes and prayed.

After breakfast, she said if we got all the work done quickly she'd tell us about Mont-de-Marsan and why Father was like the way he was.

We pulled the table back and dragged the big armchair up to the stove. We stoked up. She sat in the middle with the baby. Peter and I got on the arms. We were snug, and it was lovely. We knew Father couldn't come home to catch us.

It was an awful mess, like she'd said. But it wasn't our fault. It was no good Father hating us and being cruel. He did it, not us.

'Well,' she said, hugging us, 'I met your father, my little dears, at a motor rally. It was in 1910. It was so romantic. It couldn't have been more romantic. He was the most handsome man I'd ever seen. He was so strong and forceful. At least I thought he was. I'd never had much to do with boys. We'd been too busy. I was back at the university studying another language. I already had six. My sister and I were in all sorts of things. I was the secretary of the Students Association. I was secretary of the Beethoven Society and the Mozart Society. And the Orchid Society.

We were in practically everything worthwhile. Father was patron of most of them. Mother was on all the committees. We were very well known. Your father just swept me off my feet. I thought he was as madly in love as I was, but he wasn't. He wasn't at all. He thought he was smart and doing the best he could for himself.

'Love is a marvellous thing, real love is. It makes your eyes see only the good things in a person. If you're lucky—but you've got to be oh so lucky—your love can make that person be like that. If you're not so lucky, one day it all changes, and you see another person altogether. You see them as they really are. In *Messiah*, you know, dears, Handel's *Messiah*, it says "We shall be changed—in the twinkling of an eye." And it's true. Some little thing makes you see that person as they really are and not as your love made you see them.

'That's what happened with your father and me. My love had blinded me. When I found out what he really was, that he didn't love me at all, he was only after what he thought he was going to get through me, it was too late. I was married to him. Both our lives have been ruined.

'You know what a motor rally is, dears, don't you? It's a kind of motor race round the country. It was just before the war, and motor cars were getting very popular. Most of the haute bourgeoise had one or two. We had more motor cars in France that any other country had. That's why we had rallies. It was a lovely way of getting all the nice people together to have fun. They're not real races. If someone breaks down—and there's always someone who does—all the others stop and help them to get going again. Then off they all go, having great fun.'

I asked her what that meant, what she'd said.

'What, dear? Oh, haute bourgeoisie? Oh, that's what we were. We weren't working class. We had lots of people working for us. It means well-to-do upper class. We had butlers and housekeepers. We had other places where we lived in the winter and the spring. We had maids and gardeners and stablemen. We had all sorts. We only lived in Bordeaux for the summer season.

'Bordeaux is the coolest. It's near the sea. There's a river runs right through the city. We had yachting and boating. We went swimming at the Gironde where the river meets the sea. It's warm and you can

ANNE ANGELO

swim for hours. It's not like this cold, blustery old Cromarty Firth. And we never had to dig potatoes either. The gardeners did all that. And of course, it was never so cold.

'Bordeaux's a lovely place. There are parks with gardens and trees. You can go and stroll there and meet people. Everybody talks to everybody else. Nobody's a foreigner. So long as they're nice people, you stop and talk. And everywhere, there are masses of gorgeous flowers. And fruit trees. Everybody grows fruit. That's what you poor dears need, plenty of fresh fruit so you'll grow big and strong. We had oranges and lemons growing, and peaches and apricots. We had gardeners for the fruit and gardeners for the flowers and for the lawns and shrubs and the hothouses.

'And we had horses. We had carriage horses and riding horses. Mont-de-Marsan was our stables for breeding our riding stock. We bred all our own saddle stock. The tenant-farmers at Mont-de-Marsan were like uncles and aunts to us. My sister and I, we didn't have any brothers, loved riding. When I was as big as you, Anne dear, I'd won two pony championships. When I met your father, we'd won practically everything there was to be won on horseback. I was twenty-two, Yvonne was twenty. Our parents thought we'd never get married.

'People were different. Maybe, of course, the war's changed them. But everybody was bright and happy. The streets were full of people. Nursemaids wheeling prams and ladies with little dogs out walking. All the dresses so pretty. Nobody wears these heavy old tweeds in France. It's too hot, for one thing. And French people like bright things. And the parasols! Oh, they're the most delightful things. You just have to see them.'

Peter asked what parasols were.

'Parasols, Peter? They're like small umbrellas. They're supposed to keep the sun off, but they don't. They're too small. They're really only to have fun with and make you prettier. We had one for every different dress. You can peep round them at someone you like. Or hide behind and pretend you haven't seen someone you don't want to meet. If someone gets tiresome, you can give them a good prod and make them go away. They had hard, sharp points. They're the loveliest things. If you're good I'll make you one later on.'

She got up and changed the baby. I'd never seen her so happy. It must have been a nice place to make her look like that. Her eyes were shining and happy. She liked telling us about it. She had a kind, soft mouth. It was not thin and hard like Father's. Mother was a bit bigger than Father, but not so bony. But her hair was not so black as his. When she washed it and let it hang to dry it got little bits of ginger in it, it came right down her back, but she wore it in a bun with pins in it. Father's was getting thin, but he always kept his cap on.

She put the baby down into her cot. Then she stoked the fire. The boot-tin was getting too hot and smoking, so she put it on the hearth. We had a flat tin with fat in it that sat on the stove keeping hot. When it was time to go out to school or somewhere, Mother took the boot-tin to the door. We stepped in it with one boot, and the hot fat came up round the edges of the sole. Then when we stepped out into the cold, the fat froze, and the water couldn't get in. We never got wet feet. Mother knew lots of tricks like that.

She sat down and hugged us close again.

'Well', she said, 'it was at the end of the rally. It was a lovely afternoon. It was in the late summer. The bands were playing, and there were crowds of people lining the street. We had barricades, so they had to keep back and not get run over. There were flags and streamers everywhere. Everybody was excited. And then the first car came along. It was the Lancia. You know, the one down there in the hangar? The one with the big brass headlamps? Well, that's the same one. They gave it to us for a wedding present. It was the latest model then. A laird from somewhere here in Scotland had entered it. I've forgotten where he came from.

'It only had about another fifty metres to go, but suddenly it stopped. The co-driver jumped out and opened it up and worked on it but couldn't do any good. We saw him close it up again and whip off his goggles and helmet and run round the back and push it. Oh, my dears, the crowd went mad. They cheered and shouted. Some of them jumped the barricades to help him. The wardens stopped them.

ANNE ANGELO

If they'd even put a hand on it, it would have been disqualified. They had to do it on their own. And he was doing it too. That co-driver was your father, dears. He was marvellous. The laird was sitting inside and steering. Your father isn't very big, dears, is he? And that Lancia's a big motor car. And he pushed it right over the finishing line. But he didn't win. When he only had a few metres to go, another entry came whizzing along and beat him.

'It didn't matter, though. They treated him as if he'd won. He was the hero of the rally. The Lancia had broken down lots of times. It was too new. But he'd got it going again each time. He only got beaten at the very last. When he'd got it past the winning post, they picked him up onto their shoulders and marched him round, singing crazy songs. We all thought he was marvellous.

'And then it came to the prize giving. The winners—that was the first, second and third—had to come up onto the stand to get their trophies. I had to put a garland of flowers round their necks and kiss them on each cheek. Father made a speech and gave them the prizes.

'Everything went all right until it came to your father's turn. He let me put the flowers over his head. But when I went to kiss him, he grabbed me and kissed me on the mouth. You know, like people in love do.

'It was so bold it took my breath away. Nobody had ever done that to me before. None of the French boys would have dared. Your father was so bold and romantic he could have done anything that day, and nobody would have minded. They all cheered. I didn't mind either. I thought he was so handsome. His hair was black and curly. He had a lovely black moustache, and he was so forceful. I couldn't get away. He held me and looked into my eyes. His were so dark and bold.

'"How do you like that, eh?" he said. "It's much better, eh? You like it?"

'I didn't answer him. I really couldn't. I was too stirred up. I knew they were all watching. I knew I was blushing. But I didn't care. I was glad he'd done it. I wanted him to do it again. And that's what he did. But harder and fiercer. And I kissed him back. I wanted to. I thought he was the most romantic man I'd ever met. Suddenly, I was in love. They shouted all sorts of things and cheered.

'He said. "But you're a nice girl. I think I'll marry you, eh. What do you say? Do you think we will have nice babies? Do you think you would like lots of nice babies, eh? I'll make you happy."

'It was the boldest, cheekiest thing anybody had ever said to me. But I loved him for it. We were married in a fortnight.

'My father tried to stop me. He said we didn't know each other well enough. But I said if he didn't let us get married, I'd go off to Scotland with him anyway.

'It was the end of the summer season. Everybody would be going off to their other places. The Scottish laird was going back to Scotland, and your father said he'd go with him if I wouldn't marry him. So my father gave in. How I've wished he hadn't. I don't think I'd really have gone off like that with your father.

'It was the maddest fortnight ever. They gave parties for us every night. We were at the centre of everything. The wedding was perfect. Everybody came. There were counts and barons and judges and government ministers. We got the most marvellous presents.

'It was at the wedding breakfast that it all went wrong. If your father had only kept quiet, we'd have been away, and everything would have been all right. He'd have got everything he wanted if only he'd waited and not tried to rush things. But it was just him. It was the way he'd been brought up. He had to do it.

'He's very clever, dears. Coming from Scotland with the laird, he'd watched him and learned how to do things properly. He's always hated being poor. He'd always wanted to be like rich people, and he thought if he learned rich people's ways, people would think he was rich. We did. We thought he was one of us. Otherwise, we'd never have treated him as we had. You can't. They don't understand, and you lose control.

'My father had made his speech and given us the dowry. He told us the arrangements for our honeymoon. It was going to be lovely. There were beautiful chalets and villas waiting for us all the way to Italy. We were going to stay at your godmother's place, Anne dear, where the dinner set came from. You know, the one Father smashed.'

Peter asked her what a dowry was, and she said it was money they gave when someone got married. She said hers was a big one. It was enough to bring them right across to Invergordon and set father up in the business and still leave a good bit in the bank.

'And then the man who owned the Lancia gave it to us. He said it was a wedding present. Your father had earned it by being such a good mechanic. Nobody else could have kept it going all the way. It was the latest model.

'Your father thanked him. But he said there was still two weeks' wages owed him. He'd only been paid up to the end of the rally. Everybody stared. We'd been using the Lancia to get around in. The laird had lent it to us. When he got the two weeks' wages, he said there was another five francs for benzene he'd bought during the rally.

'That was when we found out he was only working on wages. We'd thought he was one of us. It wouldn't have really mattered, though, if only he'd loved me. But he didn't. He's always only loved money. When he got his five francs, he turned on my father.

'He thanked him for the dowry and said it was very nice but it wouldn't keep us forever. He wanted to know where we were going to live after the honeymoon. He said he wanted Mont-de-Marsan. He said he wanted our children to learn to ride.

'He'd asked me about our other places, and I'd told him. I didn't know why he was asking. He'd seen his chance when he'd kissed me like that and seen what it did to me. He'd found out that we didn't have any boys in our family and that I was the oldest girl. By marrying me, he became the oldest son. In his country, the oldest son gets everything. And he thought he was going to get everything we had.

'Father didn't understand. He said our estates didn't belong to him. He couldn't give them away like that. Your father got nasty. He said he knew his rights. There was no one living at Mont-de-Marsan except servants. He wanted it. When I tried to hush him up, he told me to mind my own business. He wasn't going to be cheated. If he didn't get it, he'd go to law about it. There was an awful scene. They were all horrified. I saw the way they looked at him. And suddenly I saw him like that too. He wasn't handsome or anything nice. He was just cunning and mean. Even the wedding clothes he was wearing didn't belong to him. We hadn't minded about that. None of the teams brought much with them. But suddenly they looked shabby on him. He just didn't belong there.

'My father saw it too. He said, "You foolish girl. Now do you see what you've done? You wouldn't listen, would you?" He was hurt. There was nothing he could do but disown me. He had to, to save the family. And that's what he did. He did it properly by law later. They put our things into the Lancia, and we had to go. I've never seen my mother and my sister since.'

'Father said it would be better for him if he took the dowry and the Lancia and went back to Scotland by himself. He said he could have the wedding presents too. He said I could stay on at home. But your father wouldn't. He said he'd married me, and I had to go with him. He wanted to get his revenge on us all by making me do what he wanted. And he thought that he would always have a chance at our estates while he still had me. And he would have done too if only he hadn't been so hateful.'

I asked her why she'd gone with him. Why hadn't she run away? We did when he was after us. She said she couldn't. It would have been too wicked.

'I'd just stood at the altar in front of them all and sworn to love and obey him until I was dead,' she said. 'I couldn't break that. Not on the very same day. I'd never have been forgiven.

'But I should have done it, though. Anything would have been better than what happened. We didn't go to any of the lovely places they'd arranged for us. We stopped for our first night in a dingy little rooming-house on the way to Calais. Your father was afraid the war would break out, and he'd be caught in France. He wanted to get back to Scotland.

'I had nowhere to run to. All my friends had been at the wedding. I had no money. He had everything. And he'd only have caught me, and it would have made it worse. I just sat there and prayed. I thought the Good Lord might do something about it for me. But he didn't. After that first night, of course, it was too late. I knew you'd be coming, Anne dear. But it was a horrible night. There was no love. It was all hate and revenge. And that's how it's been ever since. Hatred and cruelty. If he'd let us go to France when Mother died, everything would have been all right. He'd have got everything he ever wanted.'

She went upstairs and came back with the letter with the black all round its edges. She read it to us. It said her mother had died and they'd buried her. Her letter, the one I'd posted to France, had got there in time. He said her mother died asking for her. It was her father who wrote it. He said it was a pity Father hated everybody so much and hadn't let us go to France. If we'd gone, we'd have got Mont-de-Marsan. He'd promised her mother. Mother's sister was married, and they had two sons. They lived at the place in Perigueux. Nobody ever went to Mont-de-Marsan. And nobody ever went to the villa in Monte Carlo. We could have had them both. He said he wouldn't leave Bordeaux again. Everything he wanted was there. He wouldn't write again. It only made trouble and caused her unhappiness. Mother was crying when she'd read it.

And that made us cry. We were all having a good old howl. Then the clock in the parlour struck two o'clock, and Mother looked up at the clock on the mantel shelf.

'Oh my goodness,' she said. 'Just look at that time. Here we are, sitting here grizzling over spilt milk and you two poor little dears with nothing in your wee tummies.'

She got up and got dinner ready.

*   *   *

CHAPTER 4

Father's Cars

I T WAS BECAUSE of what Mother told us and what Father did that made Peter and me take a set against him. He didn't have to be so mean.

We'd never had any toys, and he had everything he wanted. We'd always thought it was our fault when he got cranky with us. But now we knew it wasn't. It wasn't anything we'd done. He just liked being cruel and nasty. No matter what we did, he was never pleased. So we set out to get even with him. My parasol was really the beginning.

Mother made me one. She always did what she promised. It was the prettiest thing I'd ever seen.

She got one of the old umbrellas from the cupboard. We had lots of them. People left them when they brought their old cars in for new ones. They left all sorts of things. There'd be money down in between the seats. We had to get in quick, or Father or the men would get to it first.

It had a carved ivory handle. It was the only straight one. The others all had curved wooden handles. She cut the ribs in half so it wasn't so big but so it would still go up and down. She took the cover off. She went and got an old dress. It was real silk. I'd never seen a real silk dress before. I wanted to wear it and play grown-ups, but she said no. People would see and think it was wasteful letting a child play in a dress like that. After she'd cut it to make a cover for my parasol, she burnt the rest. She said it was better to get rid of it. Dresses like that didn't belong in Invergordon.

She put ribbons on it so it was prettier. She showed me how the ladies in France walked and had fun peeping with them. That week while the blizzard was on was lovely. We were the happiest ever. We didn't think we'd ever see Father again.

But we did. He came while Peter and I were in the garden. We were playing Three Musketeers. I had my parasol, and Peter'd made himself a sword with two bits of stick. Suddenly there was Father coming through the hangar gate. We ran.

He was in an awful paddy. He'd got my parasol. He raved and shouted. He said Mother must be mad to make a thing like that. We could have poked each other's eyes out with it. He said she'd ruined a good umbrella, and it didn't belong to us. The people who'd left it might come looking for it, and then where would we be? Mother said it was a lot of rubbish. It had been left in the Daimler, and that had gone long ago.

He broke and broke it over his knee until it was in little bits and then he threw them on the floor and stomped on them. It was just like he did with our school things when he was cranky. Peter and I were round behind Mother, ready to run. But he didn't try to get us. He stomped off upstairs to change.

It showed us how mean he was. He hadn't been caught in the blizzard at all. He'd gone over to Leith to buy a cabin cruiser. And he'd got two new men to work in the garage. That was seven he had in there.

Mother got cranky about him buying the cabin cruiser and the Rolls-Royce and that. She only got two shillings and sixpence every week to keep the house on. He wouldn't give her any more. He said we got the oats for the porridge free, and the salt herrings came free. We could grow our own potatoes, and we didn't need anything else. Men brought the oats in sacks and tipped them into our barrels in the shed. And the same with the salt herrings. It was their way of paying Father for the work he did on their cars and boats and things. There was never much money around in Invergordon.

She waited until he was away off to Dingwall or somewhere to see his lady friend, and then she got in lots of rolls of all sorts of nice materials. She had a real sewing spree, sewing and singing away to herself, as happy as a bird. She made us all new clothes and some for herself. She made curtains for all the windows and sheets and pillowcases and great big thick towels. He didn't know anything about it until he got the bills.

We thought he was going to hit her. We were outside watching through the kitchen window. Mother backed into the corner by the end of the dresser. She was scared, but she stood up to him. He was still cranky when he'd finished, and he stomped off to the workshop. After a while, he came back and said Peter and I'd have to go and work in the garage after school. He said there was lots we could do. It would help to pay for all the things she'd bought.

It made another big argument. In the end, Mother said Peter could go, but not me. I was getting too old, and the men were too rough. It wouldn't be right. She said if he made me go, she'd go to Mr McPhee, the headmaster, about it, and she'd go to the church. Father was an elder of the church. He worried about what they thought of him. He worried about what Mr McPhee thought of him too. So he gave in about me.

It worked out good, though. We got back at him. Peter learned to ride the motorbikes and drive the cars. And he taught me. We could sneak the cars out of the hangar without the foreman knowing and go for rides. We had some lovely times. We'd wait until Father was away somewhere. And we'd try to find out which way the constable was going. We'd go off the other way.

That's how we went for our first good drive. We'd found out that the constable was going to be at Alness. That's on the way south round Cromarty Firth on the way to Evanton. So we headed north. We went right round Nigg Bay to Dunskeath Ness on the North Head of the Cromarty Inlet. We had the Dedion Bouton. We were lucky. We only got back about ten minutes before Father did. After that, we went everywhere. We'd go on the motorbikes too. Peter liked to have me on the back for ballast so he could let them out full speed. The Nortons and BSAs were big heavy bikes, and he wasn't very strong.

But Father found out somehow that we were taking the cars out. He didn't let on. But he fixed the brakes on the old Morris Cowley so they wouldn't work and I'd get killed so he could get the insurance.

Peter had taken out the James. He wanted to try it out and see how fast it would go. So I went off in the Morris Cowley. It was a lovely bit

ANNE ANGELO

of straight road, and I'd got it wound up as fast as I could. Suddenly there was a humped stone bridge with a sharp bend. The brakes didn't work, and I hit the bridge. I went out over the top and into the burn. When I woke up I was in the water up to my chin. I had an awful headache and a twisted ankle. I was so cold I could hardly move. When I crawled up the rocks and got out, I could see the Morris Cowley away across in a field. There were some aeroplanes there too. I was crawling to it when two airmen found me. They carried me into their shed and gave me tea laced with brandy. They wrapped me in a blanket and took me home. They said it was a good thing I'd hit the bridge so hard. The crumpled mudguard had acted as a brake and stopped it. Otherwise it might have kept going and cleaned up their aeroplanes. The field was all cut up too with their tailskids, and it had helped to stop the Morris. We never found the dickie-seat from the back. It must have gone into the burn and been washed away. They had a look at the brakes and said someone had taken the split pin out of the rod so they wouldn't work. It was all clean and fresh where it had been. They said it must have been done on purpose.

From something Father said, Mother guessed he'd done it on purpose. She was going to go to the police about it, but Father said she couldn't. A wife can't give evidence against her husband in Scotland. And anyway, she'd never be able to prove it. He'd only wanted to get the insurance. He hadn't known I would drive it. But he must have. The Navy wasn't due in for months and months. They only came in, in the spring and autumn. Peter said we'd fix him. We'd loosen the wheel nuts on his Rolls. But mother heard us and said it would be wicked. Somebody else might get hurt. So we didn't do it. But we kept a good lookout for anything else we could do.

The annual Highland games were coming up, and Father said I could drive the bus for that. He said if I wanted driving, he'd give me all the driving I wanted. He wouldn't let Mother get the doctor for my twisted ankle. He said there was nothing wrong with it that a couple of weeks in bed wouldn't cure.

And then it was annual games time.

I was terrified. I thought he'd fix it again so something would happen and I'd be killed. Mother tried to argue with him. She said he could see I was nearly in hysterics. He said it was only temper. If I didn't stop it, he'd give me a good one round the ears that I'd remember. He put a sign on the front: 'Sixpence a head to the Games - Cash.' He fixed a money pouch round my waist.

'And see you keep it buttoned up,' he said. 'They'll try to get their hands in it while you're driving.'

He made me get in. He put a one-gallon benzene tin behind me on the seat so my feet would reach the pedals. He showed me where the gears were. It was a great long gear lever.

'There you are,' he said. 'That's all there is to it. Just be careful. Whatever you do, don't let the engine stop. I don't want to be coming after you to start it again.'

He got out and cranked it. I hoped it would backfire and break his arm so I wouldn't have to go. But it didn't. It caught and burst into a loud rumbling roar. The gear lever wobbled madly all over the place. It was a huge thing. The houses nearly touched on both sides.

'Go on,' he shouted in the door, 'Get going. You can come home for dinner. And watch that money pouch.' He went off to the garage.

I was too scared to move it. There was only about a foot on each side where the windowsills and doorsteps jutted out. They were stone. I knew he'd go mad if I scraped one. So Peter got out and went in front, guiding me. I couldn't turn into Outram Street. I nearly scraped. So I went straight on to High Street. Peter went home then, and I was on my own.

I waited at the fountain in the High Street until I'd filled up and then went out. I was expecting all the time that something would happen. But it didn't. There were so many people out there, and the bus was so big that I couldn't turn. I couldn't go backwards. I couldn't see well enough. So I had to drive right round the games ground until I got back to the gate and out that way. On High Street it was easier. I just drove round the fountain. By dinnertime, I was getting used to it and I knew he hadn't done anything to it. I drove right down Ross Street by myself and didn't bump anything.

After dinner, I went and brought them all back again. At the end of the day, I backed it into its yard. Peter guided me. Father counted up the number of trips and the seats. He was pleased. He said I was getting some sense at last. I hadn't tried to cheat him.

'It's all there,' he said. 'You can do all the driving in future. I can trust you better than the men. And I don't have to pay you wages. It's very good.'

He didn't know I had two shillings and sevenpence tied up in my hanky in my pocket. They'd given it to me bringing them home. They'd liked me. They said I was a good kid. I was wearing a Stewart tartan costume and Glengarry. Mother had put my hair into one big plait. I usually had it in two, but she said it might get in my way and she'd made it into one fat one.

I gave Mother the two shillings. Peter and I had the sevenpence for spending money. That two shillings and sevenpence was the start of Peter and me making money. It gave us the idea.

When the fleet came in next time, Father said I could do the charter parties. Sometimes some of the officers would want to go out into the Highlands fishing or grouse shooting. They didn't know where to go, so they'd have a car with a driver. If it was on the weekends, Father would have to pay extra rates to the men. But if I did it, he didn't have to pay anyone. And they were lovely trips.

Peter and I had to be around the garage nearly all the time, hiring out the cars and motorbikes and pushbikes. We had to fill the cars with benzene before they went out. Father would carry on inside and leave it to us.

One day one of the mess stewards came and asked us if we could get some flowers. They were having a party and wanted to make it look pretty. There were flower gardens a bit out of the village. We took his money and got him some. We took them down the pier and right on board the cruiser. The officer on the gangway sent a man to take us to the officers' mess. We went through miles and miles of passages and up and down ladders. It was all clean and white. The officers' mess was lovely. I think it was then that Peter first knew what the Navy was really like. They gave us a shilling each for ourselves.

When we went for the milk next morning, we went and got some more flowers. Every morning we had to go to Mrs McKinley's. They had a cow that gave good milk, and they didn't use it all. So they sold it to us. We'd go on our bikes with a pitcher and get it.

We did the flowers up into bunches in jars with water and took them down the pier. We took it in turns. One had to stay around the garage to do the hirings and the benzene so Father wouldn't miss us. We sold them all. We got twice what we paid for them. It was good. We did it every day.

We didn't spend it all. We gave some to Mother to mind for us. She was pleased. The others at school stopped calling us 'the foreigners.' They knew we had more pocket money than they had, and they'd seen us out with the cars and motorbikes. They tried to toady up to us for rides, but we didn't have anything to do with them. Except Geordie Ross. We took him a couple of times because we were sorry for him. He was skinny and had a sore ear. He had to have a plug of cotton wool in it to stop it running. When his father hit him on it, he had to go to the doctor. He was the same age as me.

But it was the charter parties that Father missed out on. They were the best things in Scotland. He thought he was getting back at me. But he wasn't. They were lovely. I went to places and had things I'd never have had otherwise. And the officers were lovely men.

We'd be away at first light and not come back until late. Sometimes it'd be the captain and four or five officers. Six of them was a bit of a squeeze, but still fun. They'd want to go grouse shooting or trout fishing.

If it was shooting, I'd have to stay by the car so I wouldn't get shot. But if it was fishing, I'd catch a few for us and then go off for a ramble.

I found some wonderful places. Places where no one had ever been before. The mist would be lifting, and it would be all clean and new. As the clouds lightened, it would get clearer and all the colours would come up out of the ground. There'd be pale mauves and greys and blues and greens all mixing together like in a dream. It was lovely. I'd be looking down on a loch, and it'd be like a big mirror. Then out in the middle, a big fish would jump. The ripples would spread out in perfect circles until they reached the banks. And then, as if it'd been the signal, a long white finger would slant down through the clouds and travel over the water until it reached a big rock. It would stay there and light it like an altar. Suddenly it'd switch off. The clouds would quickly press down again and make it dark. And the mist would come back and hide everything. As if they knew I was watching. I was never sure if they were priests standing around or only tall clumps of white heather. The mist would come and breathe on me, all cold and clammy. As if telling me to go away. There'd be nothing to see. I'd only get soaked if I stayed. When I would go back, some other time, looking for it, it'd be all changed. I'd never find it again.

I asked Mother about it. How things could change like that, and if there really were things going on that people weren't allowed to watch.

She squeezed me against her side and said I was a funny old thing. She said not to talk about it to anyone else. They'd say I was fey. She said it's a Scots' word for people who can see things other people can't. She said I was lucky. Scotland was getting all mixed up with the French in me. She was pleased. She said most people never see the beautiful things there are in the world.

I was filling out and getting taller. Peter had started calling me slinky. He said I was changing. I was different. Mother said so too. She said it wouldn't be long before I was a young lady.

But the officers called me that. And they weren't teasing. They meant it. I knew by the way they said it and the way they treated me.

They'd always bring enough so there would be dinner for me. It would be all done up in white napkins with real silver knives and forks.

"There you are, young lady," they'd say. "You sit yourself down there and tuck into that. And there's plenty more if you'd like it."

The plates would have the ship's name and a crest. Like our good set that Father smashed. And they had proper wineglasses. I didn't have any wine, though. I'd have the pineapple juice or an orange or something like that. We'd sit around just like we were a family. And if anything got broken, there was never any fuss. They'd just pick it all up and put it in the box to go back. They were lovely men.

Sometimes they'd only want to get away from the sea. They wouldn't have guns or fishing gear. They'd have cameras, and they'd want to go away into the Highlands. I'd take them to the places Peter and I had found. Sometimes they'd all go and climb to the top. Sometimes they'd just sit in the car and look. And if a blizzard swept down on us and drove us away, they wouldn't mind. They'd say it was still worth it.

They were always fun. It wouldn't matter what happened. Even if they slipped and sat right down in the freezing water and the fish got away, they wouldn't mind. They'd joke about it all the way back. They'd make a booking to go back the next day to carry on. The destroyer men were the best. They'd be teasing each other all the time.

Father thought he was scoring, making me do those trips. I brought in good money, and he didn't have to pay a driver. And he was keeping me from school. He loved that. He didn't know, though, how lovely those charter parties were and what they taught me. They showed me what men were really like. And that showed me what he was. Although it wasn't until I tried to go to high school that we really saw how far he'd go.

*   *   *

ANNE ANGELO

CHAPTER 5

Mr Ross Is Killed

WE HAD TO leave school when we were fourteen. After that there was nothing to do but sit around until we could get on the dole. Most teamed up with someone and had babies. They didn't bother getting married. It cost too much, and they didn't think it was worth it.

I didn't want that. I knew once it started it would go on that way. I'd be stuck in Invergordon for the rest of my life. I had to get away. I had to get as far away from Father as I could. I'd look for somewhere warmer and kinder. Somewhere where they didn't worry about people being foreigners. I'd never risk getting married in Scotland. The law said you belonged to the man. He could do anything he liked with you. I'd seen how it had been with Mother. I didn't want that.

The only way to get away was to go on to high school and then maybe to university. If I were educated, I'd be able to go anywhere in the world and get a good job.

I knew father would never pay for me to go on. I'd have to get a Scholarship.

When Geordie Ross and I were thirteen, we studied for the Highlands and Islands Bursary Scholarship. For ages we'd taken it, in turns getting the Dux Medal for the best student. I think the teachers did it to make us work harder. It was a friendly rivalry. They wanted us to go on.

The trouble was with the homework. We had no place to do it. They told us to work together. We could help each other. But if we did it at my place, Father would come home early and sweep all our things off the table onto the floor and screw his dirty boots into them so they'd be spoilt. He'd tell Geordie to stay away from me. He'd only get me into trouble.

'And what'll ye do then, eh?' he'd say. 'Yer father's got nothing, and ye're only a sickly runt. I won't have it. D'ye hear me? I won't have it. You stay away from her.'

So we'd go out onto the porch. Mother would give us a lamp, and we'd work out there. But it'd get so cold we wouldn't be able to write.

If we went to Geordie's, there was always the chance that his father would come home and catch us. He'd make a fuss about me being there.

'I know what's goin' on,' he'd bellow. 'Ye'll keep at it until ye get her into trouble. An' then where'll ye be? Joe Angelo's in too good wi' the constable. I'll no' have a chance. You keep away from her.'

We were there one night. It was blowing a blizzard. Mrs Ross was in the corner by the other door, knitting. It wasn't a dole day. Suddenly the front door burst open. Our papers and books went flying. We tried to hold them down and looked. Geordie's father was there in the doorway. He was so big he didn't look real with the light on him and framed against the night. His head was still stooped, where he'd come in under the lintel. He was blind drunk and peering, trying to see who was there. The gale howled past him. He had one hand on the top edge of the door, steadying himself. His coattails and trouser legs flapped and tugged. The door bump-bumped against his boot as he swayed.

He looked awful. I grabbed things and stuffed them into my bag. He saw me.

'Aye, and there ye are too,' he shouted. 'I knew ye'd be, ye young hussy. By God, this time I'll teach ye. I'll teach ye to stay away if I have to kill ye to do it. Ye'll no' be coming back here again in a hurry. I can tell ye that.'

He let go of the door and started for me. I grabbed my bag and got under the table. It wasn't as big as ours. I had to get on my knees.

When I looked out he had hold of the door again, trying to get his balance. Mrs Ross put her knitting aside and got up and went to him.

'Come on, man,' she said, trying to take his arm. 'Let's get ye to a seat before ye fall and hurt yerself. And let's get that door shut before we lose the roof.'

'Get away from me, ye old hag,' he bellowed and shook her off. He swung a huge fist. It caught her on the side of the head and sent her across the kitchen to slam into the wall. She slid slowly down and sat on the floor. Her hands came up to hold her head. She sat there, moaning and swaying from side to side.

Geordie was still holding things down at the table. His father saw him.

'Aye,' he shouted. 'Ye're the cause of it all. Haven't I told ye to stay away from her? Haven't I? Well, now ye're for it. Come here, ye little runt.'

He made a couple of steps forward. Geordie got from the table and ran to get past him and outside. But his father caught him. Holding him by the arm, Mr Ross bashed him. He bashed and bashed at him, hitting him both ways. A hard one caught poor Geordie full on his sore ear. He let out an awful screech and fell down. Both hands went to his ear, and he screamed and screamed. His legs kicked and jerked.

His father closed in and kicked him. He kicked and kicked, using both boots. He didn't care where he kicked Geordie. He didn't know what he was doing. He was shouting things. Mad things. His teeth flew out and slid across the floor. And he kept kicking.

Mrs Ross had stopped moaning. She was holding her face but watching her husband. She said, 'He's mad. He's mad.' Over and over again. She got up, helping herself with the wall. When she was nearly up, she gave a push and ran at him. It looked like a billy goat going to butt an elephant.

Her head hit him right in the tummy. It was a big tummy. It bulged.

I thought he'd grab her and bash her, but he didn't. He didn't even try to. He stood up straighter, and his mouth opened. He looked awfully surprised. All the air came out of him. It sounded like when Father released the valve on the air-compressor when he was locking up for the night. And then he fell down. It was an awful crash.

Mrs Ross was surprised too. She thought he would belt her. She stood there looking down at him. Then she sat down on the floor by the table leg and pulled poor Geordie onto her lap and tried to hush him. She stroked his face, but she didn't take her eyes off his father.

He was flat down with one cheek on the floor. I could see his mouth and nose and one eye. It was open. He was staring at the floor. He fizzed. It looked as if all the beer he'd drunk had got churned up in the excitement and was frothing out of him. It fizzed out of his nose and mouth.

I thought I could get out. I took my bag and crept round behind him, between him and the stove. I had to step over his legs. But I couldn't get out the door. It was full of people. Their front door wasn't like ours. Theirs opened straight onto the street. They'd all come to see what was going on. I couldn't get out.

And then I noticed a funny thing. The wind had stopped. There wasn't any blizzard. Everything was quiet.

They edged in. They went all round Mr Ross and stood looking down at him. They nudged him with their boots.

'Come on, man,' they said. 'Get up. Dinna lie there like that. It's no' manly. Get up, man.'

But he didn't move. He was still frothing. It made a pool under his face and was running down between the floorboards. Someone took the lamp and put it down by his face. He didn't take any notice.

Geordie was quieter. Mrs Ross sent someone for Dr McKay. I went round picking up the rest of my things before they got trodden on. I put his teeth up on the table. When the doctor came, they took Geordie off up to bed.

Dr McKay came back down and went to Mr Ross. He still hadn't moved. It was only a minute before the doctor stood up again.

'He's dead,' he said. 'There's nothing I can do for him. Someone had better go for the constable.'

Mrs Ross came back in just as he said it. A sort of murmur went round them, and they all drew back away from her and let her through.

She went to Mr Ross and looked at him. He looked all funny and grey looking. He always had a red face. She stopped and touched his cheek. She gently touched his eye. He didn't blink.

'Oh my God,' she whispered. 'He's dead, all right.' She went down on her knees and took his hand onto her lap and fondled it. She looked up round at them all.

'I hated him,' she said. 'Oh God, yes, I hated him. But I didn't want him dead. I didn't want him dead.' It ended up in a wail. She put her head down over his hand and rocked backwards and forwards, crying, 'I didn't want him dead.' She was still doing it when the constable arrived.

They asked me what she'd hit him with. When I told them she'd only butted him, they didn't believe me. They took her away and charged her with murder.

They had to let her go, though. They couldn't prove it. In Scotland, we have Guilty, Not Guilty, and Not Proven. They said it was Not Proven.

They wanted me to go to Inverness for the trial. But Mother said I couldn't go without her. I was too young. And Father wouldn't let her go. He said she wouldn't come back. He said he couldn't go because he was working on an urgent job for the Navy.

So two men came up from Inverness. They asked me all about it and wrote everything down. They came again and asked them all again. They kept Mrs Ross in prison for over three months before they let her go. When she came home, we hardly knew her. She was so little and old and grey.

When they took her away, they were going to put Geordie into a home, but we all said we'd look after him. Every night Peter or I took his supper round to him. When we couldn't, we called over the back fence to the Kilmarnocks. Their Angus would fix Geordie. Sometimes, when I was carrying the plates round there, my hands would nearly freeze through my mittens. My feet would be numb, and my breath would turn to ice on my scarf. It was those nights taking Geordie's supper round to him that made me fix to leave Invergordon. Angus Kilmarnock was younger than Geordie and me.

They had a big wake for Mr Ross. They all got drunk. Father told us they all said what a fine man Geordie's father had been and how they hoped Mrs Ross would get what she deserved. But it wasn't her fault, not really. It was Father's. If he'd left us alone to do our homework, it wouldn't have ever happened.

I missed out on my scholarship. It was through having to go round every night with Geordie's supper and through Father making me work in the hangar. After Mr Ross died, Father said I had to go and clean and polish the hiring cars in the hangar after school every night. Mother said I was getting too old. The men were too rough. But Father said the men never went into the hangar. He said he'd keep an eye on me. And he did too.

Every afternoon, when I'd get to the hangar, he'd be there in the door of his den with his watch in his hand waiting for me. If I was late, I'd get the porridge treatment. I'd get so sick I wouldn't be able to go to school at all. And that would please him. He wanted me to fail and have to work in his garage.

He was pleased when the scholarship results came out and I'd missed. Geordie got his.

'What did you expect?' Father said. 'I knew she didn't have the brains for it. She can see the year out and then get the dole and come and do my books. It's time she was bringing something in. I'll find her a man and get her married off.'

He thought he had me all fixed. But he hadn't allowed for Mother. She tricked him although he made her pay for it. He had to leave me alone in the end. It was his own nastiness that did it. He was lucky she didn't put him in gaol.

*　　*　　*

ANNE ANGELO

CHAPTER 6

The Scholarship

I DIDN'T KNOW MY mother could fight, not until after. She'd always given in and obeyed. She said she had to. It was what she'd promised. But when she got her chance, she went after him like a tiger. She fixed him.

I didn't even know she had anything in her mind. I thought it was all finished. He'd fixed it so I failed the scholarship. He'd got me, and I couldn't do anything about it.

But she told me not to be upset. Her Good Lord knew all about it. She'd told him. He'd do something in his own good time. I wasn't to worry.

She was funny like that. Her Good Lord seemed to be with her there all the time, ready to give a hand. And he might have been too. But if he was, I thought he was more on Father's side than on mine. No matter what I did, Father always seemed to win.

The Good Lord hadn't done very much for her over the years. Father had always come out on top. If I let things go on like that, I knew I'd end up working in his garage. Once that happened, I'd never get away. I'd be in Invergordon for the rest of my life.

I was working in the hangar one Saturday afternoon near the end of the school year. Our year ended in July. I was doing the old Lancia. It was a pig. The brass headlamps were huge and took nearly an hour each. It was cold, and bits stuck out and jagged my hands. I hated it. Peter came and said Mother wanted me. He said Mr McPhee, the headmaster, and the minister, and Dr McKay were all in the kitchen.

When I got there, they told me to sit down, they wanted to talk to me. They asked me all sorts of questions. Why hadn't I been doing my homework? Why had I failed the scholarship when Geordie Ross'd done so well? Did I really want to go on to high school? Dr McKay asked if I'd like to go on to university and become a doctor. I told them why I hadn't done my homework and why I'd failed. I told them I wanted to go on to high school more than anything else in the world and I'd love to go to university and become a doctor.

They told me to go back to my work. They'd see what could be done. They said if I saw them in the hangar, I was to take no notice.

They came in and knocked on Father's door. I got into the back of the Lancia and kept out of sight.

Father was surprised when he saw them. Nobody ever came into the hangar but us. And we'd never knock on his door. He'd have gone mad. We always went round and in the front way.

'Ah, Mr Angelo!' said the minister, holding out his hand. 'And how are you this bright fine day? Well, I hope? I do trust we're not intruding?'

'Of course not, Minister," Father said. He took the hand and pumped it. 'You're welcome anytime. And I'm fine, thankin' ye kindly. Dr McKay. Mr McPhee.' He shook their hands. 'But what brings y'all here? Is it business, then? Shall we go round to my office?'

'No, no,' the minister said quickly. 'There's no need for that. It's only what ye might call a social visit. The good doctor and I were just passin' and ran into Mr McPhee here. We thought we'd look you up and pass the time o' day. Is it convenient? Have ye a minute or two? Maybe we could come in and rest our weary bones the while.'

Father was puzzled. They'd never done this before. He pushed his cap up and scratched his head with one finger. His eyes narrowed as he looked from one to the other of them. Then he stood aside.

'O' course, Minister,' he said. 'It's a pleasure. Ye'll have to forgive the place being a bit untidy. Maybe ye'd like somethin' to wet yer throats? I've got some prime whisky just up from Edinburgh.'

When the door shut, I went on with my cleaning and polishing. I'd got on to the Dedion Bouton by the time they came out. I hid again.

'Yes, well, Mr Angelo,' the minister said as they all shook hands again. 'I'm sure ye'll never regret this. She's a good girl and a fine student. She deserves the chance. The good doctor here thinks she may well go on to the university and become a doctor. There'll be room here when he retires. She'll be a credit to you and to the whole community. I know ye're goin' to be proud of her. Good day to ye, then, Mr Angelo.'

I went home and told Mother. She hugged me.

'Now you can stop worrying,' she said and laughed. 'I knew they could do it. They're lovely men. He can't go back on that. He values their good opinions too much. That's the end of it. I told you, didn't I, that the Good Lord would help? You only have to ask him and have faith.'

We heard Father's boots on the gravel.

'Out you go,' she said. 'Quickly. He might be in a temper.'

And he was. It wasn't the end of it. As far as he was concerned, it was only the beginning. He caught us in the doorway.

'Get out o' me way,' he shouted and stormed in.

'Ye think ye're smart, don't ye?' he shouted at Mother. 'Well, by God, ye're goin' to pay fer it. Did ye think I wouldn't know? That lyin' old hypocrite. Just passin' and ran into Mr McPhee here. It was your doin', wasn't it? You put 'em up to it. I'll bet ye had 'em all in here. They drank a full bottle o' me best whisky an' sat there thinkin' I was a fool as didn't know.'

He tipped his head back and glared at her from under his cap. He looked mean and horrible.

'All right, ye've got yer way. An' now ye can pay fer it. She can go to high school. An' you can get up them stairs and into bed. An' ye can be quick about it, or I'll make ye right here in front of 'em. They know what it's all about. If ye get hurt, it'll be yer own fault. The law won't help ye. Ye know where ye stand. Well?"

He put his hands on his hips and watched her. He looked awful.

I knew what he meant. It made me go hot all over. Mother's face was white. She was scared.

I ran out. I was down on the pier when Peter found me. He said they'd gone upstairs. And then I remembered the other time, when we were all supposed to go to France. I hated him. I wished I hadn't ever wanted to go on to high school.

Peter and I tried to work out ways to get rid of Father. But none of them would've worked. He was too smart, and somebody else might've got hurt. We'd have run away, but Mother had all our flower money. We'd have to go home and ask for it. We didn't know where she kept it.

We stayed until we were nearly frozen. The fleet wasn't in. There was only the old Mars over in the dock. She was a battleship the Germans had beaten up. Cromarty Firth was all rough and grey. It's generally like that. It goes mad when there's a blizzard. It comes tearing in as if it's going to rip up the piers and toss them up on the shore. Great green mountains come rushing in, their glassy sides getting higher and higher. As they get up speed, the tops slide off into white froth. The wind slices it off and flings it in your face so you can't see and your lips are all salty. We could just see Cromarty Light way out in the west. The Hill of Nigg showed darker against the overcast.

We didn't ask Mother for our money. She was too upset. She'd been crying. I told her, though, I didn't want to go on to high school. I told her I'd go and work in the garage. It didn't matter. But she got fierce about it.

'Oh no, you won't, my girl,' she said. She held my arm so tight it hurt. 'You're going on now whether you want to or not. It's all gone too far for that. What he's done might well be the end of me. The doctor warned him what might happen if I had any more children. And I'm seven years older now. Anything can happen. If it does, you two will be at his mercy. You've just got to study hard and learn everything you can. You've got to prepare yourself so you can get away. I don't want you living the life I've had. You just settle your mind to that, and no more of this nonsense. Do you understand me?'

Father thought that was the way to fix people. Make them have babies. He thought if he fixed me to have a baby, I'd have to leave school and get married. He'd be rid of me, and I'd get the same sort of misery he'd given Mother. He set his foreman on to me.

Toshack was horrible. He was at least thirty and had a face like a salmon. His upper teeth and nose stuck out, and his chin and forehead sloped back. He had little mean eyes set close together, and he was always dirty and smelly. He'd come and hang around ogling me.

'And how's my sweetie today?' he'd say. 'My, but ain't we fillin' out?' That sort of thing. I never answered him. He was too silly.

ANNE ANGELO

It was the next Saturday afternoon. I was in the hangar again. I was cleaning the inside of the Dodge. I was tired. I'd worked hard in the morning. So I got up on the back seat for a rest. I was on my back with my hands under my head and my feet up on the seat.

I heard Father come out of his den and move around. I kept still. If he'd caught me resting, he'd have gone mad. I didn't think he'd notice the door of the Dodge wasn't shut properly. And I didn't think he'd be able to see my knees. I thought the back of the front seat hid them. I heard him go back into his den and shut the door.

I must have dozed off. Suddenly Toshack was there in the doorway looking down at me. He was grinning.

'Well, an' there ye are too,' he said. 'Just like he said ye'd be. All ready an' waitin' for me. Or is it Geordie Ross ye're waitin' for? Never mind. I'm better'n Geordie Ross. He's only a boy. He's no' full grown yet. My, but ye're nice, ain't ye? How do them things come off?'

I saw where he was looking. My dress had slipped off my knees back down to my waist. I put my knees down and threw the dress to cover them. I sat up. But before I could get right up, he came in and pushed me down again.

'No,' he said. 'Don't get up. Stay there. I wanta have a look. Ye're nice.'

He put a hand on my shoulder and held me down while he pulled my dress right up.

I was wearing huggies. Peter and I both wore them. They were the only things that would keep you warm. Mother made them out of flannel for us. They were all in one piece from our wrists down to our knees. The buttons went right down the front and underneath so we didn't have to take them off every time.

He got his knees between mine and came down on top of me. He wanted me to kiss him, but I wouldn't. He was too horrible.

'Oh, come on,' he said. 'Give us a kiss. We're goin' to be sweeties. I'll be good to ye. I'll give ye things.'

My head was jammed against the end of the seat. He grabbed one of my plaits up near my head, but I could still wriggle and didn't let him.

I felt his other hand down working at my buttons, and I got scared.

I knew what would happen if I let him do that. I didn't want to have a baby. Not with him. Mother'd told me about that.

When they were breeding their horses, they had to be careful. If a bad horse got in with their blood mares, they'd all be ruined. They'd have to be destroyed. He'd leave a stain in their blood that'd show up in all their foals. It wouldn't matter who they were mated with next time—it'd still show. She said it was the same with humans. That's what's meant by 'These two are now one flesh.' It shows up in all your children. I didn't want that. Toshack was too horrible.

And besides, some of the girls at school'd had babies and had to leave. One had been found dead out in a shed behind the crofts where she'd gone and had it. People said it was the Navy, but Peter and I knew it wasn't. We'd seen cars parked where they shouldn't have been early in the mornings. They'd had frost on their windshields when we went to Mrs McKinley's to get our milk. They'd been there all night. And we knew who they belonged to too.

I told him to stop it, or I'd scream for Father.

'Don't be daft,' he said. 'He won't worry. He knows I'm here. It was him sent me. He wants us to. Now keep still till I get these buttons. I ain't goin' to hurt ye. Ye're goin' to like it. Ye're goin' to be my proper sweetie.'

I felt a button go. I lashed out at him and screamed for Father.

'Oh, stop it,' he said. 'Ye mad cat. Hush up and keep still. What's the matter wi' ye?'

Another button went. I grabbed his ears and worked my thumbs into his eyes. I dug my nails in as hard as I could. He pulled back and sat back on his heels. He tried to grab my wrists. I suddenly let go and brought my knee up and rolled over off the seat. But my knee caught him in the face.

Suddenly there was blood everywhere. He let out a howl.

'Oh, me nose!'

I was down between the two seats. I scrambled up and got the door open and ran.

'Oh, ye bloody mad cat,' he howled. 'Now look what ye've done. Oh, me nose! Oh God, me bloody nose!'

I could still hear him as I went through the gate into the garden.

Mother was hoeing the potatoes. She took me into the house and nursed me until I quietened down. Then she made me tell her what'd happened.

She made me go through it all again. She wanted to know exactly what he'd said.

'This is important, dear,' she said. 'I want to know his exact words about Father knowing he was there.'

She got awfully mad. She told me to stay just as I was. She went off to the hangar and came back with my two buttons and my hair ribbon. She kept me there with her in the kitchen.

When Peter came, she sent him back to the garage to tell Father she wanted him. Peter'd said I'd broken Toshack's nose. He'd gone off to the doctor. The other men thought it was a great joke. None of them liked him.

'And, Peter,' Mother said, 'tell him I want him straightaway and no nonsense about it.' She was raging mad.

She got the writing pad and the pen and ink and put them handy on the table. Then she started getting the supper.

Father took his time coming in. He stopped and had a look where she'd been hoeing, and finished his cigarette.

'Well, what's the trouble?' he said. He saw me and the mess I was in. 'Yes, I thought that's what it'd be. Well, there's no need to fuss. She's lucky she got away with it. She's broken his nose for him. That's what she's done. I've sent him off to the doctor. He's not the man I thought he was. It wouldn't have been like that with an Italian boy. She'd have got what she's been askin' for. She's wagged her tail at him often enough. I've seen her. It's what she wants, an' it would have solved everything.'

'Is that so?' Mother said. 'So she's been wagging her tail at him, has she? And why haven't you stopped her? You know she's underage. She's not fourteen yet. Why haven't you told me about it?'

'Why tell you when you could see it for yourself? It's plain enough. Just look at her. It's not more schoolin' she wants. It's a man. A man and babies. Why d'ye think she's been after that Geordie Ross? Get her married off. Toshack's a good man. I'm payin' him top money. I'd have seen he married her. The best thing all round. She'd be his then. Let him look after her.'

Mother held out her hand to me. I felt horrible. It wasn't true. I'd never played up to Toshack. And I'd never been after Geordie. I was hot all over. I went to her.

'Never mind, dear," she said, putting her arm round me. 'We all know it isn't true. He's just being nasty. But I want you and Peter to try to remember everything we're saying. It's important. Will you try?'

'So that was your idea, was it?' she said to Father. 'Get Toshack to give her a baby, and then she'd have to leave school. That was it, wasn't it. Make her get married to Toshack, and then she'd have the sort of life you've given me. That would have been lovely, wouldn't it?'

'I didn't say it was my idea,' Father spoke sharply. He was getting edgy. 'So don't say I did. But if it'd happened, it'd have been a good thing. It'd be the end of it.'

'Yes, wouldn't it? She'd have been disgraced, and I'd have been disgraced because it'd have been my fault. They'd all have said, "Poor Mr Angelo. Fancy him having a wife like that. And him an elder of the church." Well, it missed. And now you're in trouble, Mr Joseph Angelo.'

'I'm in trouble? What are you talkin' about? What trouble?'

'Trouble with the law. That's what. He says you sent him. He says you knew she was there and sent him in to do that to her. He says you wanted him to. Ann, tell your father exactly what Toshack said to you.'

I told him. I told him everything Toshack had said.

'There,' Mother said. 'You're guiltier than he is. She's your own daughter, and you know she's underage. There's enough to put you in prison. And I'm going to do it unless you do exactly what I say. We'll see who's going to be in disgrace, Mr Joe Angelo.'

Father didn't like it. He rolled a cigarette, but he tore three papers and spilt tobacco all down his front before he got it done.

'What's on your mind?' he said when he got it alight. 'What do you want me to do?'

'You're going to sit down here and write what I tell you. And you're going to sign it and put the date. And you're going to get rid of Toshack. I won't have him around the place. And you'll leave her alone and let her get on with her schooling. If you don't, I'm going to send Peter for the constable right away.'

'The constable won't do you any good. You can't make trouble for me. A wife can't swear against her husband. They were in it together, and you can't do anything.'

'No. I can't do anything. But Toshack can. I'll swear against him, and when they get him down there in Inverness, he'll soon tell the truth. Don't you worry. He'll swear against you quick enough. He'll try to save his own skin.'

He hated it. But he sat down and did it. When he'd done it, she tore it off and put it in her pocket.

When he asked what she was going to do with it, she told him she was going to put it in a safe place where he couldn't find it. She told him if he ever tried any tricks with me again, she'd send it to the right place.

When he went off back to the garage, Mother hugged us.

'Well,' she said and laughed. 'We did it, didn't we?'

Then she sat in the big armchair and cried.

*   *   *

CHAPTER 7

The Fleet

FATHER'S TRICK WITH Toshack did me good, though. It gave me a scare and made me keep away from the boys. It wouldn't have mattered if Rudolf Valentino himself had come along. I wouldn't have had anything to do with him.

I'd seen him in *The Sheik*. I nearly swooned when he swept her up onto his horse and galloped away into the desert. Mother spoilt it all by whispering it was a pity the pianist hadn't played some real galloping music instead of *The Blue Danube Waltz*. She said it didn't fit.

Most of the girls picked up with boys. They went and lived with them and had babies and got on the dole. I might easily have done it.

And it put me on guard with Father. I might not be so lucky next time. I knew I'd been lucky he'd picked on Toshack. Any of the other men might've been too much for me, catching me like that. I wouldn't really have had a chance.

I think he picked on Toshack because he knew how I loathed and hated him. He was so stupid and horrible. He'd have loved to give me to him. I think, though, if I'd had Toshack's babies, I wouldn't have been able to go on. It'd have been too horrible. They'd have been too much like him. I'd have had to do something about it. I haven't got Mother's faith. And then, of course, I'd have been like poor old Mrs Ross. Except I wouldn't have got off. Mine wouldn't have been an accident. They'd have hung me. And that would have pleased Father. He'd have said he'd been right all the time.

But that's where he missed out. Toshack was just too stupid. He only warned me what I could expect. I'd never be caught like that again.

I learned something else, though, that's wonderful. I learned there's a different kind of love. It's a love that doesn't mean you have to go and live with someone and do things like that. It's a love that nobody knows about except the two of you. It's sort of secret and holy. You only know it's there by the way they say things. And by the way they look at each other. And the way hands touch sort of casually and yet linger. It's a beautiful kind of love. It makes you better and happier, and oh so much stronger. You both know the other's there and willing to help if you want it. You're not on your own anymore. I made up my mind that that was the sort of love I was going to look for. The other sort, the sort that Father and Toshack knew about, was only nasty and beastly. They didn't really care.

Father didn't really care about what happened to Mother through what he'd done. We nearly lost her. Dr McKay was sure we were going to. He wanted to take it away, but she wouldn't let him. She said it would be too wicked. She'd have to go through with it. It was God's will. Dr McKay told us there wasn't much he could do. He said we'd have to pray, and pray hard, if we didn't want to lose her.

I came home from school one day. It was the first term at the high school. Mother was in bed. It was a thing she never did. She was awful. I got scared. She told me to run and get Dr McKay. She said to tell him she thought she was going to have a miscarriage. It was her tenth week. Could he come quickly. I flew.

But the sister wouldn't let me see him. She said he was too busy. I'd have to tell her. But I wouldn't, there wasn't time. I went and banged on his door until he came out. When I told him what it was, he made me drink some stuff he said would quieten me down. Then he took me home in his car.

I followed him up in case there was anything he wanted. I sat on the stairs. I heard him say, 'My dear Mrs Angelo. What on earth have you done? We'll never get you through it. I warned you last time. We were lucky then. And that was seven years ago. We'll have to terminate, or we'll lose you. Why ever did you do it?'

'Don't lecture me, there's a good man,' Mother said. She was so weak I could hardly hear her. 'Just do what you can. It wasn't my fault. He forced me. It was his revenge when you people made him give in about Anne going on to high school. After you'd all gone, he came home half drunk, and this is the result. I think maybe he knows what might happen. I think it's maybe what he wants.'

I must have fallen asleep. Because the next thing I knew, I was on my bed with a rug tucked round me. Mother was asleep too. Dr McKay had left.

He was at our place practically every week after that. Sometimes he stayed all night. And we had a nurse who came and stayed.

One day I saw Mother give him a letter.

'Here, Doctor,' she said. 'This is what I was asking you about. Keep it somewhere for me in a safe place. I don't want him to get his hands on it. If anything happens to me, I want you to open and read it and then do whatever you think you should. It's important for the girl's sake. Will you do that for me?'

'Of course,' he said. 'And don't worry about anything happening to you. It won't while you're in my care, I assure you. But why don't you leave him? This is no way to live. Go back to France or somewhere and make a fresh start. You could, you know. I expect they'd love to have you. My dear Mrs Angelo, I hate to see you like this.'

'It's no good, Doctor. I can't do it. Cruel and all as he is, I'm married to him, and he's still their father. It wouldn't be fair to them. They need us both. No. I have to go on with it, at least until they're all grown up. It must be the Good Lord's will.'

He shook his head but patted her hand. I saw the look between them.

I saw lots of things at different times. I never let on, though, that I knew. I wished he'd been my father. I'd never have wanted to get away.

I was there when he brought Father the bill after the baby was born. He made Father fairly wriggle. He knew Father hated paying out money. And he got some of his own back for the way Father had charged for servicing his car. He whacked on everything he could to get at Father for the way he treated Mother too.

'How much?' Father said, staring at the bill as if he couldn't believe his eyes. There were two detailed pages of it. 'Oh, Doctor, it can't be that much. You make a joke with me, eh? It's more than what I paid for the new car.'

Father had just bought a new Lancia, the Lamda model. He'd sold the old Theta model he'd got for their wedding present. The new one was a beauty. Peter and I had had it up to seventy-five miles an hour. Father was doing pretty well, and Dr McKay knew it.

'Yes, it might well be,' Dr McKay told him. 'Having babies is nearly as expensive as having motor cars. We're both very well aware of that, aren't we? But there it is. It's no joke, Mr Angelo. I've checked every item myself. If you'd like to attend to it now, I'd much appreciate it. I'm like yourself. I don't like putting off till tomorrow what can be done today. Better to pay when it's due.'

Father hated it, but he went off to his den and got the money. It was like taking the toffee from a little boy. Even Peter and I were taller than he was. There was a quiet smile in Dr McKay's eyes.

I was sorry for Father one day, though. It was hard to get people to work for him. They just didn't want to. I don't know whether he was too mean with the wages. It could have been.

There was a little sweet shop on the corner of Ross and Hugh Miller Streets, on the opposite corner to Mr Ogilvy's house. He had the chemist shop on High Street. Peter and I were in the sweet shop, and Mr McGrudgeon came in. We all walked back along Ross Street together. Father was standing in the garage door by the benzene pump.

'Ah, Mr McGrudgeon!' he said, coming out. 'You're just the man I've been looking for. How are those two fine boys of yours coming along?'

Mr McGrudgeon was tall and bony. He looked even taller than Geordie Ross's father used to be. They had two boys. Andrew was in my class at school, and Donald was three years older. They were all tall and bony, even Mrs McGrudgeon. Mr McGrudgeon always had a big drip shining on the end of his nose. It was a big hooked nose, like a beak with dark veins in it.

'Good day to ye, Mr Angelo,' he said and touched his cap to Father. 'Me boys are fine, thank ye kindly. But what've ye been lookin' fer me for? Can I do somethin' for ye?'

'No, no,' said Father. 'It's nothin' like that. It's the other way round. I thought maybe I could do somethin' fer you. There's a good chance here fer one of yer boys. I thought maybe it'd suit young Andrew.'

'Oh ye did, did ye?' McGrudgeon was wary. 'And what sort of a chance was that now, might I ask?'

'Well, it's like this, d'ye see?' Father said. He pushed his cap up so he could look up into Mr McGrudgeon's face better. 'My girl here, she's goin' on to the university now. She'll maybe go on and become a doctor. It's left me shorthanded. I need someone to keep my cars clean an' wash car parts an' that in the garage. Maybe it would suit your Andrew. It's good money. It'd be somethin' extra comin' in every week. Ye'd know where he was. He'd be in wi' the men and out o' mischief. An' it wouldn't affect yer dole money.'

'Aye,' McGrudgeon said. He looked at father sourly. 'I thought ye'd have somethin' like that on yer mind.' He took a step forward. Father took a step back in case the drip fell. 'I'd have ye know, Mr Angelo, that we don't need any somethin' extra comin' in every week as you call it. We manage well enough. And another thing. I wouldna want my Andrew—no, and fer that matter, my Donald either—to be in yer garage washin' car parts an' that. Neither of my lads are washer-women, d'ye see? An' I wouldna want 'em to be. No matter what the money was. I manage well enough on the dole. An' so did my father before me. I dinna want my lads to be any different, thankin' ye kindly, Mr Angelo. I'll bid good day to ye, sir." He went off along Ross Street, his drip quivering with outraged dignity.

It wasn't easy running a business in Invergordon. Father was the only maker of spare car parts in the whole of the Highlands. Parts couldn't be bought. They had to be made. And apart from that, he was getting plenty of work from the Navy Yards. He had nine men working for him.

He grabbed Peter as soon as he left school. Mother couldn't save him. But Peter loved it. He liked it so much he wanted to take a course in engineering from Edinburgh University. And that's what set us on to a new idea for making money. Father didn't pay him any wages. He said he was getting his keep and being taught a trade. By rights, Peter ought to be paying him.

We were down the pier one day. The fleet was in, and we had our flowers. A sailor came along and wanted to know where he could get some whisky. He was already half tiddly. We knew where there was a distillery about three miles out. We told him if he'd give us the money, we'd get our bikes and go and get him a bottle.

When we got back, he was so pleased he told us to keep the change. It was more than we'd paid for the whisky. So we went back and got another bottle. We hid it in the water among the flowers in case an officer or the Naval Patrol came along. The first customer for flowers who looked at all likely, we let him see the neck of the bottle. The first one that saw it grabbed it. We charged twice what we paid for it. Peter said that was fair enough. The first sailor had set the price. It was a matter of supply and demand. Anyway, he said it was all for a good cause. It was for him, so he could become an engineer and fix their ships.

In no time, we were buying it by the case. But to do that, we needed transport. So we used the cars from the hangar. We could sneak one out and be back before Father'd missed us. The old Dedion Bouton was the best. A case fitted nicely down behind the front seat. Nobody'd ever dream it was there. We kept her as our stockroom. We kept her in the back corner of the hangar so she'd always be the last one out. She was about the smallest and the oldest.

It was a lovely way of getting back at father. Peter said it was poetic justice father should provide us with free transport and benzene. He said if Old Scrooge had paid him his proper wages, he wouldn't have needed to go sly-grogging.

I didn't like him calling it sly-grogging. It sounded too wicked. But he only laughed.

'What's it matter what you call it? It's the same. It's a good community service. They need it. We can get it for 'em. It's the same as if it was eggs or cheese. There's nothing wicked in it.'

But a guilty conscience is a powerful thing. You can never tell when they're going to trip you up and land you in trouble. Mine did. I was always afraid, Father being an elder of the church, that someone would find out and there'd be an awful row. I was always on edge while we were doing it.

I came back up to the garage one day. It was a Special Fleet Review Week. The base was full of ships, and our whisky was going like hotcakes. I'd just taken two more bottles to Peter down along the pier. There were only two left. Then we'd have to go and get some more. I was working out how many gallons we were going to get through and how much we were going to make if it kept up like this. Standing by the garage door was Lord Louis Mountbatten. His photo had been in the papers a lot. He was in full dress uniform, all white and gold. He had his hands on his hips and looked annoyed.

'Come on, young miss,' he said. 'Get a move on. I'd like ten gallons please.'

I nearly burst out laughing. I thought, 'Ten Gallons! Golly, what a party someone's going to have. The whole fleet will be tiddly. Ten gallons in one pop. Wait till Peter hears about that. We'll have to go and get it for them.'

I walked on air.

'Yes, sir,' I said as I got closer. 'That'll be all right. We can do that for you. More if you want. The only thing is, though, you'll have to wait a wee while. We'll have to go out and get it for you first.'

'You'll have to what?' His eyes narrowed, and he looked at me intently. 'What do you mean? You'll have to go out and get it for me. Go where? Haven't you got any in the pump?'

And then I saw the big black Bentley standing there. I felt myself going red.

'Oh, you mean benzene?'

'Well, what else do you think I meant? Whisky or something? What else do you sell by the gallon up here?'

It was his 'whisky' that did it. Why would he mention whisky if he didn't know? He must have known and he'd come to catch us. It was only a trap. They were probably down there now grabbing Peter. They'd take us off to prison. I wished I'd never even done the flowers. I thought about what it was going to do to Mother. And how Father would crow. He'd love it.

I looked at him, and he was altogether different. He was like the figure of doom standing there. I thought,'As soon as I've filled him up, he'll make me get in and take me away. I'll probably never even see Mother or Peter again.' I felt so miserable I could have howled.

'Hey, hey,' he said. 'Watch what you're doing. I want it in the tank, not all over the ground.'

I hadn't put it in properly, and it was squirting back. When it rang up 10, I stopped and put the hose back in its rest and waited for him to tell me to get in. When he didn't, I looked at him and said, 'Well, there's your ten gallons, sir.'

'Not according to my gauge it's not,' he said sharply. 'Have a look for yourself. It says only 9, and there was a bit in there before you started. You didn't put that much on the ground. I want 10, not 9, miss. I'd like my other gallon please."

It was too much. Now he'd get me for selling him short. I burst into tears. I hadn't meant to cheat him. I'd forgotten to prime the pump. It was a hand pump. It had to be primed before each sale. It took a gallon to prime. I'd been so flustered I'd forgotten.

'I'm sorry,' I sobbed. 'Please, I didn't want to do it. But it's for Peter. So he can be an engineer.'

'What on earth? Oh, come on, young miss," he said. 'It's not as bad as all that. I'm not going to cart you off to prison or make you walk the plank or anything. Just give me my other gallon, there's a good girl. I want to get along.'

As soon as he'd gone, I raced down the pier looking for Peter. He was still there on the edge coaming with his jars of flowers. I told him to throw the whisky over the side. They'd be here any minute.

'Can't,' he said, grinning like mad. 'I've already sold 'em. I'm having a field day. Whizz back up and get the other two bottles. But what's wrong, Slinks? You've been crying. Your face is all tear stains. Here, bend down.'

I had to wet his hanky with spit. He wiped my face while I told him what had happened.

'You're a big dope, Slinks,' he said. 'We're not doing anything wrong. It's only your guilty conscience. I bet they've known all along. They'd have to. Someone would tell 'em. I'll bet His Nibs is sitting in a mess room somewhere right now enjoying a good snifter of our whisky. It's prime stuff, that. The best tonsil-tickler in the whole of Scotland.'

'There now. You'll do.' He put his hanky away. 'Now off you go and fetch the other two bottles. The admiral himself'll be along in a minute. I told him I'd keep him two. Then we'll have to go and get some more."

Peter was getting impossible. I couldn't do anything with him any ore. Since he'd been working with the men in the garage, he didn't seem scared of anything.

That Special Review Week was marvellous for us, though. We sold more than ten gallons. It's funny how things turn out. Each bottle held a quart. Twelve to the case made it three gallons. We got through three cases and six bottles. I learned another good lesson and got away with it. And I'd found out what a guilty conscience can do.

Peter was catching up to me. He was nearly as tall but thinner. He said I was changing too. I was different. He stopped calling me Anne or sis. It was always Slinks or Slinky. I liked it. I knew I was different. I knew by the way the Navy men looked at me and the way they spoke when they came for hirings. They thought I was nice. I saw them admire my hair.

It was long enough so I could sit on it. I mostly wore it in one plait tied with a big pink butterfly. It was black like Mother's except when I'd washed it and had it loose to dry. Then it had coppery glints. I usually wore a two-piece jacket and skirt in the Stewart tartan with a matching Glengarry with good long ribbons. Lots of the girls wore the Stewart tartan. It had to be a woollen blouse because of the cold, black stockings, and brogues.

Those three years in high school were lovely. Dr McKay was good to us. He often came around. He'd always come along and talk over the fence while his car was being serviced. He used to bring us things. And Father left me alone so I could do my studies.

We had one nasty scare with him, though. We thought he had us.

It was over our whisky selling. The Fleet was in. I came back up for more bottles. When I got to the hangar, the Dedion Bouton was gone. Father had hired her out to two officers to go fishing. We didn't know if he'd got our whisky. There was nearly a full case. Or whether the officers would get it.

He didn't say anything, and we couldn't ask him. All we could do was hope. And hang around so as to be there when they came back.

There was a bare chance they mightn't see it. And they might see it and not touch it. They'd almost certainly mention it when they came back. We had to keep them away from Father.

There was a chance they might see it and whizz it down to their ship before coming back. But we didn't think they'd do that. They were always too decent. If it wasn't there when they came back, we'd be pretty sure Father had got it. He'd glory in it. It'd be a Christmas present. We'd just have to be there when they came back and try to find out.

We hung around the garage door all day. Father came out several times to see what we were up to. He'd watch us for a while and then scratch his head and go back inside again. But it could have been an act. He could have been laughing up his sleeve at us.

As soon as it came in sight, Peter whizzed into the garage and kept Father talking. I grabbed it and shot it into the hangar. I told them I'd fix their deposit up when I got back.

It was still there! That was a lovely sight. We didn't know whether they hadn't seen it. Or whether they'd seen it and decided it wasn't any of their business. They could easily have done. We didn't mention it. They were lovely men. Different altogether from the men in the garage. They all were, from the ratings to the captains, commanders and admirals. I never had such lovely times as I did on those charter parties. They taught me what men could be like.

*   *   *

CHAPTER 8

Apprentice With The Chemist

BUT IT WAS all wasted and hopeless. I was a fly kicking and struggling in Father's web. He had me, and he knew he had me. He'd only bided his time. I didn't see it until my final exams. People asked me what I was going to do when I got through. I hadn't thought that far. But I had to face it.

I was seventeen. I didn't have enough money to get away. All our whisky money had gone for Peter's engineering. I didn't know anyone or any place outside of Invergordon. I didn't know anything. Oh yes, I knew how to sell flowers and whisky to sailors. And I knew how to wash and polish motor cars. And how to drive them. But who'd want that? I'd done well in high school, but being good at French and Latin wouldn't get me a job. Anyway, there weren't any jobs to get. There was only the one. The books in Father's garage. And I'd have to take it.

I couldn't sit around the house. It would be no use asking for the money for my university fees. He'd never meant for me to go. It had been only talk. He'd let me have my dreams. He'd let me work and study and kept out of the way. He'd had to. But he'd only bided his time.

Things had changed. Three years had gone. He was safe on that score. If Mother brought it up, they'd want to know why she'd kept quiet about it so long.

If I didn't take his job, he could even stop me getting the dole. He'd say he'd offered me a job and I wouldn't take it. He'd be all innocence. I'd be branded as a loafer who didn't want to work.

Toshack was gone. But that didn't matter. He'd have somebody else in mind. And I'd never know how or when. As the weeks shortened to days, it grew into a nightmare. I couldn't sleep. I couldn't eat. I lost weight.

It got me down so much I even began thinking I'd been wrong. I should have picked up with one of the boys. Most of the other girls seemed to be doing well enough. At least they had someone they liked. Most had a baby or two. They had somewhere of their own to live and someone to look after them. I had nothing. I was still at Father's mercy. Even Toshack would have been better than this. It would have been over and done with.

But it had its own cure. Mother got so worried she sent me to Dr McKay. He put me on a tonic. I had to go to the chemist to get it made up. Mr Ogilvy, the chemist, asked me what was worrying me and what I was going to do when I left school. I didn't tell him everything. I think Dr McKay had been talking to him. He seemed to know an awful lot. He offered me a job as his apprentice. The wages wouldn't be much, but when I was through, I'd be able to sit for the exams and become a fully qualified chemist. I'd be able to go anywhere in the world and get a job. It would be a three-year apprenticeship. It was like the gates of heaven opening to me.

When I told Mother, she said I was a silly old thing.

'Why don't you have more faith?' she said, stroking my hair and smiling. 'You're such a silly old thing. The Good Lord made you, didn't he? And hasn't he looked after you all right so far? Why do you have to worry so much? You're a big silly. You think you know it all, but really, you don't know a thing. He works in ways you'd never dream of. Now stop your worrying. Everything's going to be all right.'

Father wouldn't sign the papers until I agreed to pay him the two shillings for my board. I only got two shillings and sixpence a week for the first six months. But I didn't worry about that. I was on my way. Nothing was going to stop me.

They'd looked at me differently when I started in high school. They looked at me differently again now. I had a job. I had a good job. I was going to be a chemist. The girls brought their babies in to me for advice. Then the differences showed up. I was always neat, my hair done with a ribbon. I had a clean starched white smock every week. If I had an accident, I could put on a clean one straight away. When they came in, most of them were dowdy, even slummocky, in curlers and tatty clothes. They didn't really know anything about their babies and what was wrong with them. I was thankful I was me. I was someone important. I'd have hated to be in the messes some of them were in. And it was all through their own ignorance. At least that's what I thought.

Mother saw it differently. She said I'd only been lucky. It was the things that had happened to me that had made me like I was. It wasn't all my own doing.

I had to laugh when she said I'd been lucky.

'What? I've been lucky to have had a father who hates me like he does? Lucky he set Toshack on to me like he did? I don't call that luck. I think I was lucky I got away.'

'Yes, dear, you were,' she agreed. 'But if things hadn't happened to you like they have, you and Peter, you wouldn't be like you are. You've had to stand on your own feet and learn to fight. You've had to get out and earn your own pocket money. You can both run rings round the others. Look at you. You walk straight. You look straight at people. You think straight, and you talk straight. You're clean and nice. You're not like some of the poor things you went to school with. You tell me about them yourself, coming into the shop. You're good-looking, you know, dear. I don't want to make you conceited, but you are. You're very good-looking. When you decide on your man, you won't find it hard to win him. You just stay as you are and be thankful.'

The boys thought so too. They hung around the shop like the moths round the lamp up on the pole outside. Mr Ogilvy didn't mind. It was good for business. They mostly bought something or other.

They all vanished when Geordie McPhail showed up. It was in my second year. Geordie had been the policeman ever since I could remember. He'd be in the shop for an hour to an hour and a half two or three nights a week, thinking up things to talk to me about. After he'd gone, Mr Ogilvy would come out from the dispensary and ask what he'd bought this time.

'Afraid that won't do him much good either.' He'd smile and shake his head. 'Not for what ails him. What on earth does he do with it all?'

ANNE ANGELO

But Geordie McPhail was very good for me. He showed me rocks I hadn't known about. He set me up on the highest pinnacle. And then smashed it down and rubbed my nose in the dust.

He had a nice tenor voice. He'd come and sing to me under my bedroom window. I admit I liked it. If he'd only kept going that way, it might have ended differently. I'm not saying it would. I'm only saying it could.

Being a part of Father's select card-playing circle, he knew when Father was away. Then he'd come and serenade me. Maybe he thought that was the way wooing was done. His two favourites were 'My Love Is Like a Red, Red Rose' and 'Ye Banks and Braes o' Bonnie Doon.' When he came to the bit in 'Ye Banks and Braes' where it says 'And my false lover stole my rose / and, Oh, she left the thorn with me,' Geordie put his whole heart into it. It would echo back from the houses opposite. I don't know what the neighbours thought. He must have kept them awake.

One night Mother thought it might be too much for me and came in. I was at the window peeping through the curtains. A great cheese of a full moon was poised over the chimney pots listening to Geordie at his wooing.

'Don't you let him see you there,' she whispered urgently, 'or you'll never get rid of him. He'll know you're interested, and it'll make him bolder. If you give them the slightest encouragement, they think you're only playing hard to get.'

'I wish I had a red, red rose,' I said. 'Like they have in the operas. So I could toss one down to him.'

'Don't you ever do anything of the kind,' she said. 'Nor a hanky or a bit of hair ribbon. It'll be fatal. You'll never get away from Invergordon. He'll take it that you return his love. One night he'll grab you and put the pressure on. He'll think that's what you want. Geordie McPhail won't be any Toshack, my girl. He's powerful. He can go into the hotel and toss out the biggest of them on his own. You'd better stop leading him on and put him out of his misery. This is cruel and heartless.'

But it wasn't. Not really. He must have been enjoying it, or he wouldn't have done it. And it was romantic. I thought it was lovely.

He was the village's best catch. Mrs Geordie McPhail would get lots of concessions others wouldn't get. She'd be a well-respected person. She'd be looked up to. And she'd certainly be well looked after. I know I liked to hear him down there.

But he came to the boil too soon. He was waiting for me one night. The shop only had the one door. He insisted on walking me home. He had to talk to me alone. He wanted us to go down along the Shore Road where we could look at the sea. We went along King Street, which runs parallel to Ross Street on the other side of our block. When we came to Hugh Miller Street, I turned along it. I told him Father would be waiting for me. I couldn't be late. He said Father knew and wouldn't worry. That rang little bells for me. When we got to Ross Street, I turned up it and made for our gate.

At the gate, he did his best to get hold of my hands, but I kept them both firmly on my purse. He tried to keep between me and the gate, but I sidled past. So he got desperate and blurted out what was on his mind.

'Och, bonnie lass, I canna do wi'out ye.' He was almost in tears. 'It's jist no good. Yer father says ye're a bit of a tiger, but I dinna care. I canna live wi'out ye. Say ye'll be mine, bonnie lass. I'll be good to ye. I swear I will. Ye'll be the happiest lass in Invergordon. If only ye'll say the word.' He was trembling. His hands fumbled for mine. I was thrilled. I'd never dreamed it would be like this.

'O' course,' he urged, his voice breathy, 'I canna offer ye marriage. Make no mistake about that. It's me mother. She'll no' let me. She says it wouldna do. You bein' a foreigner an' that. But dinna worry. She'll come round when she sees the sort o' bairns we have. She'll have to. They'll be her gran' children. What do ye say, bonnie lass? I'll give ye everythin' yer heart'll want. Och, we'll be so happy. I swear ye'll never regret it.'

I burst out laughing. I couldn't help it. It was either that or slap his face. And Geordie McPhail was far too big to risk that. I was still laughing when I shut the gate behind me.

'Och, dinna laugh, bonnie lass. It's no joke. Ye're breakin' my heart. Dinna go, bonnie lass. Come back. Come back.'

Father was waiting for me in the kitchen.

'What's happened to you?' he said. 'Why do you look so happy?'

ANNE ANGELO

I didn't tell him. Geordie could if he wanted to. I wondered how much scheming they'd done. I wondered what he'd told Geordie about Toshack's broken nose. It did me good, though. It brought me down to earth. I might have a good job. I might be going to be a chemist. But underneath it all, in their eyes, I was still only 'the foreigner'. It brought home to me what I'd been in danger of forgetting. I had to get away from Invergordon. I had to get away from Scotland. I had to find some place where I could get married without belonging to the man body and soul. I'd been so wrapped up in my studies and work that I'd forgotten the purgatory of my mother's life. It was having its effect on her health.

Dr McKay was treating her for diabetes. He said it was the result of years of unhappiness and bad food. He was very good to me during my apprenticeship years. He helped me with problems. He lent me books on anatomy and physiology and coached me in them. He even covered up my one serious mistake.

He came in one day with one of my bottles in his hand. He was serious, but there was a twinkle in his eye.

'Is this yours, young lady?' he said, holding it out to me. It was. My initials were on it. It was a laxative I'd done during the week for Angus Kilmarnock. It was Angus who'd helped with Geordie Ross while Geordie's mother was away in Inverness Prison.

'Yes,' I said. 'It seems to be. It's my signature. Why? Is there anything wrong with it?'

'Look at it,' he said, holding the bottle out to me.

I took it and read it.

'The Mixture. Angus Kilmarnock. Take four every two hours.'

'Well? What's wrong with that?' I said.

'If you'll look in your prescription book', he said, 'you'll find I prescribed two every four hours. That's just a quarter of what you've made it. You've got the poor boy worn to a shadow. His mother's quite upset. What, are you settling an old score or something? You can dump that lot. He doesn't need any more.'

He went out laughing. And I don't think Mr Ogilvy ever knew. Dr McKay was a lovely man.

He'd taken a much greater interest in me than I'd thought. He came bustling into the shop the day my apprenticeship finished; round behind the counter, picked me up off my feet in a great big hug and kissed me on the forehead.

'There,' he said. 'Congratulations. You've done it. How does it feel? Bruce! Come out here and congratulate our new chemist. Today's the day.'

'Good gracious,' Mr Ogilvy said, coming out taking off his glasses. 'So it is. My word, how time flies. You did a good thing there, Donald. She's been the best I ever had. When are the exams, Anne?'

I was breathless. It suddenly dawned on me that I'd really done it. The door was open, and I was on my way.

'In a fortnight, Mr Ogilvy. The application has to be in next week. I'll need to be down in Edinburgh for a week for the exams.'

'You'll fly in,' he said. 'With what you've learned from me and all that physiology and stuff from Donald here, you're a certainty. You can't go wrong.'

For that week. I walked on air. Then I filled in the application and went to Father for the money. I'd need fifty pounds to cover my fees and board for the week. It was too far to come home every night.

He wouldn't give it to me.

'D'ye think I'm mad?' he said. 'Fifty pounds? You must be out of your mind.'

Fifty pounds didn't mean all that much to him. He was doing well. He had ten men working for him. He'd just bought himself a cabin cruiser. He didn't like the motor that was in it, so he bought a Rolls-Royce sedan and put its motor into the boat. Then he bought a new Dodge and put its motor into the Rolls. Father could do anything with engines and motors. He and his Rolls-Royce and cabin cruiser were the envy of Invergordon. They all said he must be a millionaire. But he wouldn't give me the fifty pounds for my exams.

Mother went to him.

'You've got to, Joe,' she pleaded. 'You can't do this to her. She's worked hard and got through. She'll pay it back if that's what you want. Anyway, you've had more than fifty pounds out of her wages since she's been working there.'

Every time I got a rise, Father put my board up so that I only had the sixpence. I could never have done it but for Mother and Dr McKay. They were wonderful to me.

Father said it wasn't the money so much. It was me going down to Edinburgh by myself. He said I'd be in trouble in no time. He wouldn't let Mother go with me. He said she wouldn't come back. And he certainly wasn't going with me. Anyway, it was all a lot of rubbish. There was a good job waiting for me here in the garage. I ought to take it and stay here with the family. It was where I belonged.

Mother went to the minister, but he wouldn't help.

'I'm sorry, Mrs Angelo', he said, 'but I canna help you this time. It's no' my business. Your man's right. Edinburgh's no place for a young girl to be on her own. They're a sinful lot. He's her father, and he's right to have a care for her. If I interfered and anything happened, it'd be on my head, and I canna have that. There's signs o' backslidin' already. Both in her and in your young Peter. They've both stopped comin' to church and Sunday school. It's been a year an' more. No. I'm afraid you're goin' to have trouble there. I can't help you.'

Peter and I'd stopped going because of the hypocrisy. It was just after Father'd had to get rid of Toshack. It'd been his turn as elder to read the Lesson. The fleet had been due in the next week, and he'd stood up there in the pulpit and ranted, 'Lock up your wives and daughters. The evildoers will soon be among ye. There shall be a great weeping and a-gnashing of teeth. Beelzebub shall triumph.' And they'd all chanted, 'Allejuia. Amen!' As though it'd been the Navy that'd caused what had happened out among the crofts. We just didn't go back again.

Dr McKay came and had a go at Father, but it was no good. He wouldn't budge.

'Thank ye for your interest, Doctor,' he said. 'But she's my daughter, an' I know what's best for her. Down there on her own, she'll get into trouble and come back with an unwanted brat. So don't think you'll be helping by lending her the money. She's not going, an' that's all there is to it.'

There was still one chance. Peter had gone to Edinburgh to fix up about his engineering degree. He'd taken all our money so Father wouldn't be able to get his hands on it. He was going to buy books and pay his fees and book lodgings as far ahead as he could. There was a chance I might catch him before he spent it all.

I sent him a telegram care of the university office, but he never got it. He was already on his way home.

When he got home and told me he'd spent everything he had, I realised how hopeless it all was. Whatever I did, Father would win. I went upstairs and put on a coat and scarf, warm mittens, and a tam. It was a fine drizzle, but I felt I had to get out of that house. I had to get away from Father. Somewhere where I could be alone and think things out.

I remember going past the church as they all came out from Sunday school. I turned away from them. I couldn't have stood that. I got down along the pier. Everything was cold, wet, and grey. We have long grey twilights in the Highlands. The pier was grey and empty. The sea was grey and lonely. As far as I could see, away out to Cromarty Head, there was nothing. Even Cromarty Light was gone, hidden in the grey misty drizzle. The sea heaved and rolled as if it too was unhappy.

I sat on the stringer along the side. I got near a bollard to get some shelter and to have something to lean against.

It seemed to me the sea was watching me. As if it knew I was there and wanted to help me. Right down where the grey became green, it seemed to be waiting. It seemed friendly. It surged up as if trying to be near and comfort me. I thought of the sailors going into it when their ships went down. It was clean and nice. It would cushion them. It would be cold, and it would soon be over. Then they'd just float away, and nobody would be able to do anything nasty to them anymore. Nobody would ever know where they'd gone. I took off a mitten and reached down. I wanted to see if it was really so cold, what it felt like. It came up to meet me but didn't come high enough. I reached down farther. I knew it was down there, right down deep, watching and waiting. I'd have to reach down farther.

*   *   *

ANNE ANGELO

CHAPTER 9

The Position Vacant

'ANNE! ANNE! LOOK out!' It was Peter's voice. It was a long way away, but it was Peter's voice, shouting.

He'd be all right. Peter would get along. Nobody would try to do anything nasty to him. It was going to come up again. This time it would be all right. We both knew; it was going to be all right this time. I stretched down to meet it.

Suddenly I was grabbed. I was grabbed and pulled up to my feet. Two arms tight round me, held me.

'Oh gosh! Gee whiz, Slinks! What on earth are you doing? You were nearly in!'

It was Peter. My face was against his shoulder. He was wet. He hadn't got a coat. I realised I was crying.

'Golly, you're soaked,' he said. 'This is crazy. You'll get pneumonia. Oh, come on. Let's go home. I'm frozen. I've been everywhere looking for you. It's late. They've been back from church for hours. This is no good. Come on. Let's go home.'

Poor Peter. He almost had to carry me. I didn't want to go, and I was so cold I could hardly walk.

They made me have a hot bath. Mother gave me extra blankets and brought me hot milk with some of Father's whisky in it. It was awful stuff, but it made me warm inside.

Dr McKay came to see me. It was a week later. After he'd checked me, he sent Mother out, shut the door, and came and sat on my bed.

'Now look here, young lady,' he said, taking my hand between his and holding it. 'This is just no good. There's nothing really wrong with you. You've just got to snap out of it. There's nothing to be afraid of, and nobody's going to hurt you. You're a big strong girl, and you've got everything to live for. Something will turn up. It's not the end of the world. Think of your mother. She's got quite enough worries without you going on like this. I'm surprised at you. Really, I am."

After he'd gone, Mother brought me in some *London Times*. They must have come from Mr Ogilvy. He got them regularly. She said we'd go through them. There might be something in the advertisements.

And there was. It was a few days old, but it still mightn't have gone.

> Governess wanted. French family, two boys and two girls requires the services of a governess/tutor. Must have good French, English and Latin. Apply with recent photograph and copies of two references to advertiser, 241 Rue Nationale, Lille, France.

If only it hadn't gone, it was made for me. I got a photo taken and references from Mr McPhee the headmaster, Mr Ogilvy, and Dr McKay and sent them off. I gave my address as care of Mr Ogilvy's shop. He said I could, and Mother said it was a good idea.

For over a week, I stewed. And then it came. I'd got it. They would meet me at Lille Station. I had to send them a telegram from Calais. To me it was like the gates of heaven opening. And then Father slammed them. He wouldn't give me the money for my fares.

'So that's it, eh?' he said. 'I know there's something going on. First you want Edinburgh, and now you want France, eh? What's the matter with you? Why do you want to send her away, eh? Tell me that. You think he is better for her than her own Papa, eh? Well, she's not going. I'm her Papa, and I say she stays here. This is where she belongs.'

Mother showed him the advertisement and the letter.

'So what's the difference?' he said. 'Maybe it's right, and maybe it's only a trick. I don't care. She's not going. Why would she go over there, eh? I'll give her a job here. In the garage. It's a good job. I'll find a good man for her. She'll be happy where we can help her. Over there she wouldn't last five minutes. No. She's not going.'

But he gave me the money. He didn't know he was giving it. I bet he got awfully mad when he found out. But he gave it.

It happened through Peter. Mother said it was wonderful how the Good Lord did his works. There was enough for everything and a bit over for pocket money. Peter said a man came into Mrs MacPherson's shop and gave it to him.

'I was in, buying a couple of exercise books,' he said. 'This man came in and gave it to me. He said to give it to you. You'd know what to do with it. Honest he did!'

Mother had to get cranky with him before he would tell us the truth.

'It was Dr McKay,' he said, grinning with glee. 'He came in and asked when Anne was leaving. I told him she wasn't. We couldn't get the money for her fares. He told me to stay there. He'd be back in a minute. When he came back, he had this and father's account for the last service on his car. He said if I'd receipt the account and put the date, and if Mrs MacPherson'd initial it as witness, I could take it. It'd save him a trip to the garage. He said to give it to you. He was sure you'd know what to do with it. He went off as pleased as punch. He's a wizard.'

'A wizard?' Mother said, smiling as she put it in her pocket 'Oh my dears. You don't know what a lovely man he is. He's just the loveliest man ever. Oh, but doesn't the Lord work in wonderful ways?'

She crossed herself. 'I wish I could make you two have more faith. Can't you see how it works? Oh, but what's Joe going to be like when he finds out about this?' She laughed happily. 'Never mind. Come on, Anne. There's packing to be done if you're going to be on that train tonight.'

I knew how she saw it. She thought her Good Lord had worked on Dr McKay to make him do it. And she might have been right. But it seemed to me Dr McKay did it himself. He liked us and didn't like Father. He knew what an Old Scrooge he was and saw a lovely chance to put one on him. But whichever way that was, there was something else nobody knew about but me.

Happening in the morning like it did made all the difference. If it'd happened in the afternoon, I'd have got away quietly. Father wouldn't have known. But as it was, there was a row. And Peter won. I didn't really have to go. It was only Mother and Peter that made me. It's odd how things turn out. You can never do what you want.

We were up in my room. We were so busy we forgot the time. The first thing was Father, in the doorway, home for his dinner. There was no mistake what was going on. Mother's best suitcase was on the foot of my bed. There were things all over the place. She was folding them and putting them in.

'What's going on?' he said. 'I thought I told you she's not going. Where's my dinner?'

Mother gave him a quick look but kept on packing.

'She is going, Joe,' she said quietly. 'She's got to. She can't let them down now. She's going on tonight's train. But I'm sorry about your dinner. I'll come down and get it for you right away.'

Then she said to me, 'Here, dear. You carry on here. Fold them nicely so they don't crease. It's going to be a tight squeeze. There's a lot to get in." She pressed my hand and whispered, 'Don't be afraid. Everything's going to be all right.'

But I was afraid. I was scared stiff. He was cruel. There was no telling what he'd do. It was all so utterly hopeless. Whatever I did, he always blocked me. It would have been better if it'd ended down on the pier. I picked up a pair of huggies. I was going to pick up everything and put it all back in the drawers. I knew it was hopeless.

'Stop that,' he said. 'I told you you're not going. Put all those things away before I give you a good beating. I'm your Papa, and I say you're not going. Go on. Put them away!'

'You won't give anyone a good beating.' It was Peter. He'd been along in his room, studying. He came in and stood beside me, facing Father. 'Not while I'm here you won't. Go on, Slinks. Get on with your packing. He's not going to stop you.'

'You keep out of it,' Father shouted. He had his fists clenched. 'Or I fix you too. You're getting too big for the breeches.' He watched Peter from under his cap.

Peter told him to stop it. He said he was getting sick of his ranting and going-on. If he was going to fix him, he could get on and try it. But to leave me alone. Peter was terrific.

Father stood and looked at him. Then he said, all right. We could both go. We could go right now. He wouldn't have us in his house. But he said if we took anything that didn't belong to us, he'd have us put in prison. Peter told him to go away. It wasn't his house. It belonged to all of us. He'd bought it with Mother's dowry. We were going, all right. But we'd go when we were good and ready. Suddenly I wasn't scared either. We had a new master in our house. The future was going to be lovely.

* * *

CHAPTER 10

France

IT WAS NEARLY time to go. I was all packed and dressed. Mother and I were sitting on my bed talking. Peter was along in his room. Father was in the garage. I had on my best two-piece costume and Glengarry all in the Stewart tartan. My shoulder bag was the same, and there was a matching tartan rug strapped to the outside of my suitcase. I had a royal blue blouse in hand-knitted double wool. Peter had bought me a beautiful Cairngorm to hold it at the throat. My warmest tweed topcoat in beige and my scarf were lying on the suitcase. I'd taken the ribbons off the Glengarry. They made it look too childish. I'd had my hair cut too. It was my first ever. Mother had been horrified. But I'd had to. I looked too much like an overgrown schoolgirl. Mrs Kilmarnock had made me warm woolly mittens to match my coat. I had hand-knitted Stewart stockings. My feet were snug in stout black brogues. Mother said I looked nice. She'd given me her Robbie Burns. She'd put a sprig of white heather in it from the clump under the old pear tree at the back of the house.

'It's not much, dear,' she said. 'But it's all I have that's really my own. I bought it soon after I met your father, when I knew we'd be coming to Scotland to live. I wanted to learn all I could about it. I've put a bit of heather in it for luck. It's a lovely sweet clean thing. I hope it'll help you to keep that way.'

I asked her about men. I didn't know anything. There'd only been the boys coming into the shop. And Toshack and Geordie McPhail. I asked her if they were all like that and how I'd know when the right one came along.

'No one can tell you who's the right one, dear,' she said. 'Not even your heart. It can play tricks on you. Especially in the middle of your month. That's when you're most emotional and likely to be attracted to a man. It's Nature's way. She's like that with all her creatures. She wants you to mate then so you'll have a baby. You have to hold back. You have to fight yourself, and you'll have to fight him too. Everything will urge you on.

'If you give in, it can lead to disaster, not happiness. You'll be starting something that'll take at least eighteen years to finish. It'll be that long before your child will be able to care for itself. Lots of men, when they find there's a child coming, will fade away. They won't want you. They'll think you were easy with them, you'll be easy with the next. Think of the girls you told me about coming into the shop with their babies. Do you want to get like that?'

I didn't. Some of them had got themselves into awful messes. They were younger than I was but had already lived with two different men and had babies by them. They'd made out they were happy, but underneath it all, I'd known they weren't. They'd been worried stiff.

'It's not easy to bring a child up on your own,' she said. 'You've got to have money. And you can't be out earning it and looking after your child at the same time. Your child needs a father. Life will be a misery for both of you. And if you do manage to get another man, he's not likely to have the same affection for your baby its real father would have. He'll want children of his own. He'll give them preference. But why would a man want to saddle himself with a secondhand family? There are plenty of good single girls about. They'll find one and move out to marry them. You'll go from one to another, getting cheaper and cheaper. That's the way so many girls end up on the streets. Oh my dear, I don't want that for you. There are diseases that can make you wish you'd never been born.

'You have to make your head rule your heart. Take your time. It'll be for all your life. Remember what I told you about our breeding horses at Mont-de-Marsan? Once a mare was mated with a bad horse, she was finished with? It would show up in all her later foals? It's just the same with humans. The first man you mate with will show up in all your later children. It'll be in your blood.

'Watch him and see if he has the qualities you want in your children. Is he cruel or kind? The shape of his features can tell you a lot. And so can the way he is with animals. They know.

'The shape of the mouth can show you. Kind people don't have cruel mouths and cruel, people don't have kind ones. Lots of men wear moustaches to cover their mouths. Often you'll find it's a cruel one. And moustaches show they're vain. If you ask them why they let that bit grow, they'll tell you it does something for them. What can it do? Why do they need something done for their faces? There must be an inferiority complex. And there's surely vanity. If he wasn't vain, he wouldn't spend so much time fiddling with a few whiskers. The man who's strong and busy either lets it all grow and trims it like a haircut. Or else he shaves the lot off and is done with it.

'There're lots of things tell you what a man's like. The way he walks. And stands. The way he looks at you. The look in his eyes. The way he talks and moves his hands. The sort of clothes he wears and the way he wears them. The vain man wears narrow, long-pointed shoes he can't even walk in comfortably. He can be too natty and dapper. Some men are effeminate. You don't want that. It's the woman who should be feminine. The man should be masculine and sure of himself. That's what makes the attraction between man and woman. The differences. You don't want your boys to be prissy sissy things. That's what they'll be with an effeminate father. It'll not only be in the breeding, it'll be in the example he gives them as they grow up. You don't want that. You want your boys to be boys, to grow up strong, self-reliant men able to look after and fend for their wives and children. You want to be proud of them.

'Your father's hard and cruel, but there's nothing prissy or weak about him. Look at you and Peter. You can both run rings round the ones you went to school with. You can look after yourselves. It hasn't been all my doing. Some of it was in the blood. Your father's hard life as a child may well have showed up in the way you and Peter got out and made yourselves money with your flowers and whisky. There was never any of that in our family. There was no need. But the need was in his and may well have been the cause of you two doing so well. I often wondered about that.'

'What do you mean?'

'Well, dear. It's a remarkable thing he never tried to find out where Peter got the money for his engineering courses. He must have known he'd got it from somewhere. He'd have known it couldn't have come from me. He never gave me enough for that. It wouldn't have been remarkable if one of the sailors had asked him where the kids were that sold the whisky. It would have happened at some time. Your father would have caught on. He's quick.'

It reminded me of the Dedion Bouton and our case of whisky stashed in the back. He might even have known about that. I'd never seen him in there. But being the good mechanic he was, he'd likely have been in to check the cars. If he had, he'd likely have seen it. He'd have known it must have been ours. I wondered if he had.

'Look at Peter this morning,' she said. 'How many boys of eighteen could have stood up to a grown man like he did? He was willing to fight for you. Joe must have known it. Maybe he let him get away with it. I'm not saying he did, but he could've done. I've never understood him. And you too, you've got a backbone in you. Look how you came through with Toshack and Geordie. It could have been very different if you hadn't been like you are. You learned from that. You'll know what to do if you're ever caught like that again.

'Men will try that sort of thing. They'll try to get you away on your own. They'll try to get you to drink things so you'll be all warm and happy and give in to them.

'Try to find out what he wants from you. Does he only want to satisfy his hot passion? That's all a lot of them want. They think it's clever to make someone submit. But it's not. They give you their baby and then go off and don't care what's happening to it. It's a part of them, and they don't care. What sort of a man's that? Why, even the animals care and fight for their young.'

I asked her if Father had ever tried to make her give in to him.

'Oh no, dear,' she said quickly. 'There was never anything like that. He was too clever. I thought he was being noble. It was one of the things that made me like him so much. But he wasn't. He just wasn't after me. He only wanted to get married so he'd get our properties. There was no love for me at all.'

I told her she shouldn't have gone with him. She should have stayed there at home. She could have got a divorce. And she said it's what she should have done. It would have been better. But it had seemed too wicked, on the very day of her wedding.

'I was only young,' she said. 'I'd been brought up very religiously and taught always to do the right thing. I should have got away and left him. I know that now. I should have jumped out and run. But I didn't. I'd been taught to have faith. So I only sat and prayed. Afterwards, of course, it was too late. I knew you'd be coming. It's what I'd planned. I wanted to have his baby, to belong to him and be a part of him. I didn't know it would be you, of course. But I knew there'd be one.'

I said I understood that, but it really wasn't what I'd meant. I wanted to know about love. How do you make love? What did I have to do? I didn't know anything.

'You don't make love, you great silly,' she said. 'It's not a thing you can make. It's a thing that happens naturally between a man and a woman. Nobody can teach you. It's better if you don't try to learn. You should go to each other fresh and unknowing. You learn each other's ways with no memories of anybody else to spoil it. He does his man things to make you happy. And you do your woman things for him. Nobody can tell you about it. You find out from each other.

'It starts with a look in the eyes. You each see something in the other you like. Something is said or done. It's liked. And it's answered. And the answer's liked. It'll grow. You each explore the other. As you talk, you find you're not afraid of him. You meet and go out together. That first liking develops. You eat together. Liking grows to affection and trust. You touch each other. You put your arm through his, and you're proud of him. And he's proud to have you do it. You mean more and more to each other, and other people and things mean less and less. You find you're so different and yet so much alike. It used to be called courting. It's a lovely thing. Everybody liked to see a courting couple. Love grows and unfolds gradually. It's a tender, delicate plant.

You think about him. You dream about him. Especially in the middle of your month. The longing to be with him is almost unbearable. I told you that's the most dangerous time. If you want this love to be yours and keep growing, you have to fight against yourself and it. You'll have to fight against him. He'll be feeling the same as you are. He'll be fiercer. But if you want it to last, you have to wait until you're married. It's the only way for lasting happiness. For the sake of the children you'll have and for yourselves, you have to go into the church in front of them all and do it properly. If it's real love, you'll be proud to. Remember, children of unmarried parents go through life with a handicap. There's a nasty name that's never forgotten. It's not their fault. It's the fault of the parents.

'You get a home and make it a place of love. You each try to imagine what the other will like. You do everything you can think of to please him. Think of everything he might need. And into this world of love your babies are born. The father develops in fatherhood. The woman in motherhood. In this little world of your own, you love and care for each other and for the tiny lives that are part of each of you. Oh my dear, it can be the most beautiful thing. Love is meant to be the greatest treasure we can have. But it must be cared for. Yes, and planned and waited for.'

'Yes, I know that,' I told her. 'But can't you tell me what to do? What did you and father do? I don't know anything.'

'My dear girl', she said, shaking her head, 'can't you understand? There's never been love between your father and me. I did love him, yes. I loved him madly before we were married. But since then, it's only been sufferance. I've had to submit because he's stronger and got the law on his side. But there's been no love.'

'But you've had four children. You must have made love to do that.'

'Making someone have children, dear, isn't love. Lots of children have been forced on women without any love. Where there's real love, there's no need for any making or forcing. You're both willing, eager, and yearning. You're both on fire with it. It's been growing since you first met. Believe me, dear, when your wedding night comes round, you won't need any coaching or lessons. You'll know what to do. Stop worrying about it.

'There's another kind of love too,' she said. She gave a sad little smile and sighed. Mother's smile never was a very happy one. She'd never really had much to be happy about. And her diabetes wasn't getting any better. 'It's a love that's not like that,' she continued. 'It hasn't any of that hot fire. It's a gentler, more steadfast sort of love only wanting to help and be kind. It's a nobler kind of love, really.'

I knew what she meant. I'd seen it. It was beautiful. But I asked her if she'd ever known of a love like that. She said she had. But by that time, she'd had two children and expecting a third. Nothing could be done about it.

'But that's enough talk,' she said, getting up suddenly and bustling about. 'It must be nearly time you were going. You'd better go and say goodbye to your father. At least you owe him that much.'

I understood. I felt sorry for her. He was a lovely man. I hoped I'd meet someone like him. It was the first time she'd ever let on.

I didn't want to go near Father. I knew there'd only be a row. He was always against anything I did. But she insisted.

As soon as I went into his office, he picked on me. He started on my hair.

'So', he said, 'what did you do that for, eh? Now you look like a real hussy. Did she make you do it?'

I told him I'd done it myself. It made me look too young.

'Too young?' he said. 'You're crazy. You've always been crazy. It was the best thing about you. No matter. It's done now. So what do you want? You've come to say goodbye, eh? You're going?'

I told him I was. I held out my hand to shake hands with him, but he grabbed it and grabbed my arm. He held me so tight it hurt and took me out by the benzene pump.

'Now you listen to me', he said, shaking me roughly, 'and you listen good. If you get on that train, you don't come back. You understand? Not ever. You're not my daughter anymore. I finish with you. You understand? You're not bringing a baby back for me to look after. You get a baby, you fix the baby yourself. You get married, that's different.

But you get into trouble, and I don't know you. OK? Now, if you want to go, you go. Go on!'

He gave me a shove that nearly made me fall. He went back inside, and I heard his office door slam.

Suddenly it was all flat. Instead of looking forward to it, I didn't want to go. There wasn't any need, really. With Peter like he was, there'd be no more trouble with Father. I could stay. The exams would come round again, and I could do them then. The fleet would be in again, and we'd get some more whisky money. I'd get a better job as a chemist than I would as a governess. And I wouldn't have to go all the way to France. There'd be plenty of jobs in England. The more I thought about it, the more miserable I got. When I got there, the children might not like me. The people might not like me. I might not even like them. And then I'd have nowhere to go. I wouldn't be able to come home. As I walked along to the hangar yard, I made up my mind. I wouldn't go.

But I didn't get a chance to tell them. They had the Dodge out, with the motor running. They were all in it waiting for me. Mother and the girls were in the back with my things.

'Come on, Slinks,' Peter said. 'Hurry it up, or we're never going to make it.'

It sounded as if he wanted to get rid of me. When I looked at the others, they looked away. As if they all felt the same. They wanted me to go. Everything froze inside me. I got in and didn't say anything. It was the same all the way. No one spoke. It was horrible. Like being taken away to execution or something.

It was the same at the station. They were all edgy. They wouldn't look at me. They just stood around and fidgeted. And then it was a rush. Peter found me an empty compartment. It was a sort of duty hug and kiss all round. They put me in and shut the door. And then I was going, and they were still there. They all seemed suddenly happy and pleased, waving and shouting things. It was horrible.

Before we were really out of the station, I was in a corner having a howl. I hadn't wanted to go, but they'd made me. There was only Father who hadn't wanted me to go. And it was all his fault I'd had to. They must have all been fed up with me and hadn't said so. I wondered who'd get my room and all my things. I wondered if Father would forgive me if I got off and went back.

I had a chance. I would have done it if we'd been at a station. But we weren't. We were in the middle of some yards. I thought we must have broken down. There was a lot of shouting and clanking. But we were only getting another engine.

'It's all right, love,' he said. He was carrying a lantern. 'Dinna worry. We're just givin' ye another engine to get ye up over the Grampians. Sit ye doon and relax. Ye'll be on yer way in half a jiffy.'

The Grampians are the mountains separating Scotland from England.

Every minute of that night was a misery. Those two engines howled and shrieked like demons gloating that they were rushing me off to some horrible fate. As soon as I got comfortable and dropped off, they'd wake me. I ate Mother's sandwiches and wrapped up in my rug, but it did no good. When I had to change trains, I asked only men in uniform. Mother had warned me about that. And I didn't bother with any refreshments. I didn't dare risk missing my connections.

At Calais I sent my telegram and found my train. And it was a good thing I did. I'd never have got on it otherwise. They packed in like sardines. They were either all one family or all from the one village. Everybody knew everybody, and they all chattered madly. And they all smelled of manure and garlic. They had piglets done up like sausages in wickerwork, with only the snouts and tails sticking out. They put geese and chickens up in the racks, tied together by the feet in twos. The heads hung down. They swung. They swung in rhythm as if to hypnotise me. A pink eyelid would go up, and an eye would peep. To see how I was taking it. Knowingly, the eyelid would slowly come down again. And they'd all go back to swaying. And then another peep. I had to stop looking. Stringnet bags of onions, potatoes, and carrots filled every space.

But the worst thing was the great fat bottom in the calico dress that bumped and rubbed itself in my face. It seemed deliberate and didn't miss a chance. I couldn't move to avoid it. I wondered if it wanted my seat. It couldn't have sat in it anyway. Maybe it just didn't like me. As

ANNE ANGELO

the heat built up, the farmyard stench grew stifling. There wasn't a window open. I was afraid the geese in the rack over my head might do something and it would fall on me. I took off my Glengarry and kept it under my coat. It would be horrible meeting my people with something like that on it and not knowing. If it fell on my hair, I'd know and be able to clean it off.

To take my mind off things, I thought I'd improve my French by listening to their chatter. But I couldn't understand a single word. They could all have been Greek or Hebrew for all I could tell. I panicked. If I was on the wrong train, I'd never be in Lille at the right time. I'd never be able to find them. I had only three shillings and sevenpence in my purse. It was an awful feeling. In a strange country, alone, not knowing where I was or where I was going, and no money.

And then someone moved, and I saw 'Etat' stamped into the seat leather. At least I was on a French train. But I couldn't tell what the stations were. They shouted something, but I couldn't hear what. And I couldn't see. My view was limited to the calico dress with its great bulges and the swaying chicken heads.

Suddenly everybody grabbed things and piled out. We were in Lille. I sat back until they'd all got away.

It must have been the smelliest, grubbiest station in all of Europe. Even the steam from the engine was putrid. As I got level with it, it belched a vile cloud that engulfed me. I'd been hot since I got off the boat at Calais. By the time I got clear of that steam, I was soaked in perspiration. It ran down my face. My hair was in wet rat tails. My clothes clung to me. I stopped and took off my heavy overcoat. It was hot, and I thought I'd be better with it off. I didn't know who I was to look for. Nor where I was to look. I thought I'd get out in the middle and stand there. They'd be able to see my Scottish clothes and might recognise me. That's partly why I'd worn them. That, and they were my best. And I thought if that didn't work, I'd look for a policeman, a gendarme, and show him my letter. I thought they'd be sure to help. But carrying my coat was hotter. My arm was wringing wet in no time. I'd had to keep my scarf and mittens on. There was no room in my shoulder bag.

I was through the ticket barrier. I stooped to pick up my case.

'Ah, good,' said the voice right beside me. 'So you found your way all right, then, Miss Angelo.'

I looked up. He was tall and clean looking. He was about forty or so. Much like Dr McKay, but a bit older and more prosperous. It was in English. It flustered me. I was trying to think in French.

'Bon dieu, mam'selle!' he said before I could say anything. 'But you look hot. Par bleu, yes! Here. Give me the suitcase. Oui, and the overcoat too. We do not want you to melt. Non?'

That was the second lovely relief. I'd found him. And I'd got rid of that wretched suitcase. Maybe I was going to be all right. He was friendly. And he was thoughtful. He had smile crinkles round his eyes.

As we walked through the station, I took off my scarf and mittens and carried them. I got out a hanky and wiped my streaming face and squeezed the ends of my hair. I asked him how he'd been so sure it was me.

'It wasn't very difficult,' he said. He looked me up and down and smiled. 'I was looking for someone from Scotland. If you're not from Scotland, I've never seen anyone who was. You only need bagpipes and the little bag thing that hangs down in front, and you'd pass for Bonnie Prince Charlie himself. What is that—is it a costume you're wearing?'

I told him it was the Stewart tartan. Lots of people in Invergordon wore it. Lamely, I said I'd thought it might help in finding him.

'And have you got the bagpipes and the little bag?'

It made me feel good when I saw he was teasing. People only tease when they like you and feel friendly.

But it was the car that really did it. It, and the way he opened its door and put me in. It was the biggest, blackest, and shiniest car I'd ever seen. An American model left-hand- drive Buick. It was the last word. It wrapped itself round me in luxurious comfort. Even father's Rolls-Royce hadn't felt the same. A huge load fell away from me.

*   *   *

CHAPTER 11

My New Home

B UT THE DRIVING was crazy. They were like maniacs, whizzing madly all over the road and all going the wrong way. The streets were wide but jam-packed. People missed death by inches and didn't even know it. Great juggernauts of tram cars rumbled through the middle dinging their bells and hurtling on. It was utter chaos and bedlam.

'So you drive, do you?' He was amused. He glanced down meaningfully at my feet and then at my hands. I realised I was stretching down full length, my feet reaching for the brake that wasn't there. My hands were clutching my shoulder bag tightly to me as I braced, waiting for it to happen. I wondered how long I'd been doing it. And how long he'd been watching me. It was horrible.

'Yes, I do. But not like this. I've been driving since I was eleven. But this is crazy. There's no need to go so fast. And you're all on the wrong side of the road. Someone'll get killed.'

'Yes,' he said, and his smile broadened. 'I suppose it does look like that. I suppose tram cars are strange to you too. They're villains. But you'll get used to them. It's good that you drive, though. Could be very useful. Here, give me this.'

He took my bag and put it on the seat between us.

'It'll be safer there,' he said. 'The way you're treating it, you'll have it in pieces any minute. Now sit back and relax. We're not going to kill anyone. If you can't bear to watch, close your eyes. It's not far. We'll be there in five minutes.'

And then I enjoyed it. Stores and shops gave way to big blocks of houses. I saw Rue Nationale up on a corner post and remembered the name from the address on my telegram. It seemed to be a main boulevard. The houses looked affluent and expensive.

We stopped at one that was a palace in stone and marble with ornate balconies and delicate ironwork. It towered up three stories. From the parapet, stone faces of demons and gargoyles grimaced and glared down.

'This is it,' he said. He got out and came round and let me out.

There was no fence or garden. It stood hard against the footpath like a fortress.

The small dormer windows above the gargoyles would have been the servants' quarters, or maybe for the children. Behind them rows of tall chimney pots stood up against the skyline. The second floor had wide French windows and balconies with room for a dozen people. A tracery of ornate ironwork curlicued up round them. The ground-floor windows had stout iron bars that could have kept out the Revolution. The entrance was like a gaping cavern and reminded me of Stirling Castle. A semicircular fanlight over the top made it even more imposing. Massive mahogany doors with a raised pattern of six-inch squares in rows were folded back along the inside walls.

It was so grand I felt out of place. I didn't belong here. I was suddenly conscious of my homemade clothes. Of the bright tartan colours and my heavy brogues. All the people in the streets were dressed in the latest fashions and all light, summery things. I saw them turn and look at me. I felt there were people, elegant people, peeping down at me from behind those second-floor lace curtains and whispering. I wished someone had told me it was going to be like this. I'd probably ruined everything. I'd been mad to have come.

He'd been watching me. He came closer.

'Yes,' he said. 'It is big, isn't it? But it's quite nice inside. I think you'll like it.' His arm touched along my shoulders. 'But come on. Let's go in and meet them. They're not a bad lot, really. But you'll have to be firm. I think you'll be all right.'

I felt I was entering a castle too. With those doors shut, no one would get in or out. A rabble could pound on them all night with no effect. Ten marble steps went up to plate-glass doors. Everything was

ANNE ANGELO

spotless. We'd started up when I remembered my suitcase and coat. I stopped to go back for them, but he said not to worry. They would be attended to.

Going through those plate-glass doors was breathtaking. It was like entering a cathedral. A huge foyer went up the clear three stories to the roof. The roof was stained glass. The sunlight coming through bathed everything in rosy pink. A grand staircase curved up from left to right around the far wall. The bannister and supports were in gold and continued round the first-floor landing. And then on up round to the second floor. The walls, all the way up, were cream tiles. It was gorgeous. It made my neck ache. Hanging from the roof centre, a magnificent chandelier sparkled and shimmered like a huge diamond. There must have been a thousand crystal droplets. The floor had an intricate pattern of black tiles among cream, one that made a stark contrast. Against the wall, in the curve of the stairs, a large mirror reflected the mass of flowers in front of it. 'Breathtaking' was the only word that could describe it.

A woman came through a hallway on the left. She was about Mother's age, but better groomed and better fed. She didn't look as if she'd ever had to dig her own potatoes. The dress was elegant. Her hair had been done in a salon. She had rings on her fingers. She was poised and confident.

'Ah, good, Marie-Louise,' he said in French. 'This is Mam'selle Angelo. We'll be up in the bureau. Let the children know, will you, please? And there's a suitcase and overcoat in the car. See they're brought in. Where have you put her?'

'In the Louis the Fourteenth, m'sieu. I thought it would be best. It's closest to the children and the stairs. Is that all right?'

'Yes, indeed. Excellent.' His French was easy, but hers was too fast. I wondered if he was doing it purposely.

'Marie-Louise is our housekeeper,' he said in English. 'Anything you want, any problems, go to her. She's a jewel. Well, come on, then.'

He went across and up the stairs.

It was delicious. My feet sank into it, like walking on air. It was a deep soft pile with a floral pattern. The bannister was perfect.

Before we reached the first-floor level, an opening on the left showed steps going up to a dark-panelled door. He went up and opened it.

'Come in,' he said. 'This is my bureau.' I followed him in. 'I'm usually in here when I'm home. These are my rooms. But I'm away quite a lot. You can meet the children in here. It has a quietening effect on them. They can be lively. Nicole's the one. Win her and you'll win the rest. She's fourteen. Therese's seventeen and suffering from a bad attack of puppy love. Jacques is twelve, and Gilbertee's five.'

It would have subdued and quietened anybody. It was a world of comfort and seclusion. It was the sort of study they'd have at Number Ten Downing Street or at Buckingham Palace. Nothing had been spared.

He went away through a door on the right. I stayed where I was. My brogues had cleats that could drop dirt. I'd forgotten to clean them coming in. I'd have hated that. It was the same lovely carpet as on the stairs, but in a lighter shade.

The soft gleam of well-polished walnut set the tone. An enormous desk with its telephone and a leather chair pulled up close dominated everything. Bookshelves and cabinets stood back from it. Deep-seated dark-red leather chairs added their sombre tones. In an alcove nearly hidden by bookshelves, a brown divan in velvet with silk cushions waited. There was a phonogram there. Through muslin curtains gently billowing from wide French windows, I could see out to a spacious garden with patches of lawn showing among tall shrubs and flowerbeds. Beyond there were glimpses of a high brick wall. Heavy brocade drapes, held apart by big bows of ribbon, could be released at a touch to fall and shut the world out. A war could go out there, and in here would be peace. It was a man's domain. His 'There are my rooms' and 'Marie-Louise is our housekeeper' and 'Anything you want, any problems, go to her' came to my mind. I wondered where Madame the wife was.

He came back wiping his hands on a small towel.

'Here they come,' he said.

It was like the sound of waves breaking ever closer along a pebbly beach. They flowed up and in through the door. They were all redheads, but all different shades. The bigger girl's was shoulder length. The smaller's was in a thick plait with a green ribbon. The little fellow had a mop of pale-gold curls. They rushed to be first to their father.

The girls were the first to turn. I was surprised at their figures. Even the younger one was better developed than I was. I wondered if French girls matured earlier. They were wary and took me in from Glengarry to brogues. I had my scarf and mittens in my hands with my shoulder bag.

'Well, here we are then,' the father said. He spoke in French, but it seemed to me he took care so I could understand. 'This is Mam'selle Angelo. You all know who she is, don't you? She's come to look after you and improve your English. Do you still think she's an ogre, Nicole?'

He ruffled his hand on her head and smiled when she looked up reproachfully at him.

I couldn't follow the string of rapid French she fired off at him. I guessed she was objecting to what he'd said. But I wasn't sure. I knew if I made a mistake at this stage, it could well spoil everything. I remembered what he'd said about being firm. I didn't know how much English they had, but I took a gamble.

'Yes,' I said in English. 'And that's all very well too, Nicole. But I don't blame you if you said I looked like an ogre. It wasn't a very good photo, was it? Do you understand what I'm saying? All of you?'

I spoke carefully and slowly, and they all nodded, except the little one. He was too busy hugging his father's legs and wanting attention.

'Good,' I said, and I meant it. If they were as good as that, it was going to be much easier than I'd thought. 'That's fine. Your father wants me to improve your English. I think we may as well start right away. While we're together, we'll only speak in English. We'll get more practise like that. Will you try? It won't matter if you make mistakes.'

Again they all nodded. And they were relaxing. They weren't so wary.

'All right, then. Now how about you, Nicole? How about telling us in English what you just said to your father about ogres? Go on. Have a try?'

She made a little moan and looked to her father for assistance but he laughed and told her to go ahead.

'Go on,' he said. 'Mam'selle Angelo won't eat you.'

'It is not zat I say you are ze ogre, mam'selle,' she said slowly. 'It is only zat I say ze,- how you say, ze photographie—it is like ze ogre. Zat is what I have say to Papa.'

'Yes, and that's pretty good too,' he said, laughing. 'That's about what you did say. Very well, then. So we stick to English. Now this is Therese.' He put a hand on her shoulder. 'Nicole you know already. This is Jacques. And this little bundle of mischief is our Gilbertee.' He swept him up, hugged him, and set him down again. 'So now you all know each other.'

'Now suppose you girls take Mam'selle Angelo—by the way, what is it? What do you like to be called?'

'Oh, it's Anne,' I said.

'All right. So suppose you take Anne up and show her where everything is? She's in the Louis the Fourteenth. But don't be too long. It's getting close to dinner.'

Then he said to me, 'Don't bother changing. You won't have time.'

He was pleased. He'd wanted me to succeed. With him on my side, and I felt I'd got the children, there was only the mother left. I was doing well.

Following them down onto the main stairs, I saw across the foyer and down out to the entrance that those huge wooden doors were shut. There'd be no going in or out. I was in a fortress. But a beautiful fortress with everything in it I could possibly want. And I'd been accepted. It was a lovely feeling.

The room they took me to was fantastic. It was like stepping straight into French history, or something out of Georgette Heyer. It was the first from the stairs on the first floor. Theirs were adjoining.

Like a vision in rose and silver, it was so utterly feminine it simply breathed romance. It could have been a room for Marie Antoinette or Josephine. The French windows and balcony were like in *Romeo and Juliet*. Cream tulle curtains in a crossover style gave it a personal, intimate air. Heavy drapes in blush-rose brocade, held back the same as in his study, would guarantee restful sleep. The bed was smooth luxury. A rose-satin eiderdown gleamed softly through the lace bedspread. Elegant with silk cushions, a hand-carved chaise longue stretched invitingly. The exquisite Louis XIV writing desk was romance itself. Somewhere there simply had to be a secret drawer. A secret drawer with long-faded love letters from the King to his mistress. Letters smelling faintly of perfume and pomade. The dressing table matched it in perfection. Delicately curved legs and fragile wing mirrors with the fine gold filigree brought to mind elegantly wigged gallants with huge lace ruffles breathing hotly on coquettish necks.

A door by the writing desk opened to a perfectly matching bathroom. Everything was there, even huge cakes of scented soap at the bath and hand basin. The taps were silver and gleamed like the towel rails. Gorgeous thick cuddly towels and a monster rug by the bath waited for me. The floor was blush-rose tiles. It was my own private bathroom.

I remembered what he'd said about not changing. It puzzled me. I went to the dressing table and carefully arranged its mirrors so I could see myself from all angles. But I couldn't see anything wrong.

'Is it zat you make it yourself?' Nicole had been with me all the time. Therese was still at the window gazing down onto the street. 'You are wanting to see if it is fitting, oui?'

'No, not quite, Nicole,' I said. 'Yes, I did make it. Mother and I did. But it's not that. I wanted to see if there was anything wrong. Is there? Does it look all right?'

'Oh, but yes. It is nice. I like it. But you must be clevair to make sings for yourself. And you are lucky. You have ze mamere. We do not have our mamere. Le don dieu, He take her away for himself. It is sree years now she is gone. Marie-Louise, she is our mamere now. She is good, but it is no ze same. She is too busy. She has too many ozzer sings to do.'

That was the moment I saw it all clearly. There wasn't a thing to worry about. They needed me here. He didn't want a governess to teach them English. He could've done that himself. His was perfect. And anyway, theirs was good enough for what they'd want. What he wanted was someone to look after them and be company for them while he was away. The housekeeper couldn't do it. She was too old and too busy with her other things. It needed someone like me about their own age but old enough to keep control. I'd been the leader of our Sunday school group at home.

I wondered if he'd had somebody else and they'd let him down. I thought he must've done it, in three years. It could be why he'd wanted someone different. Why he'd got me from Scotland. He must've had plenty of answers. Suddenly I was glad I was me. I was proud I'd worn my Stewart tartan. I wouldn't let him down.

I saw Nicole differently too. She wasn't a rich girl I had to try to win. She was just a poor kid feeling lonely and missing her mother. She envied me because I had mine and because I could do things. Probably Therese was so caught up with her love she never even gave her a thought. She looked so wistful and pathetic. I wanted to put my arms round her and give her a good hug. I wanted to tell her not to worry, I'd look after her. I'd be her friend.

But I didn't. I thought she might resent it. It was too soon and might drive her away. I had to go slowly. And she had to come to me.

'Yes, well, I'm sorry about that, Nicole,' I said. 'But I'm afraid I'll have to go and have a wash and brush up now. I don't want to be late for dinner."

I was so hot and sticky I would have loved to have got in that gorgeous bath and soaked and soaked and gone without dinner. But I knew I mustn't.

I'd sluiced my face and hands and done what I could with my hair. I was checking the cleats of my brogues when the soft booming of the gong floated through.

Nicole put her head in the door.

'You must come quickly,' she said. 'We have to go. Albert does not like it for us to be late.'

'All right, Nicole. Be with you in a minute.' I wondered who the Albert was. I didn't think it could be her father.

I caught up with them going down the stairs. But I was a very different me from when I came up. I knew now what it was all about. And I knew I could do it. A door had opened, and a door had closed.

Invergordon and Father with his porridge and salt herrings, Toshack and Geordie McPhail, and the freezing blizzards were gone and finished. I was the governess. I was taking the children down to dinner. I held my head up and walked straight. I wished I'd had bagpipes.

*   *   *

CHAPTER 12

Settling In

I T WAS COMING out of that dinner I needed a skirl on the bagpipes. It was a disaster. I made an absolute fool of it. With all the lovely food there was, I came away starving. And to put the currants in the gingerbread, I thoroughly tramped on the butler's corns. He was the Albert everybody was so much in awe of. But it had to happen like that. If it hadn't, I'd never have got through to the others like I did. It was only through winning Nicole first.

It wasn't a dining room. It was a banqueting-hall. There were three long tables. One went down the centre with a smaller one on either side. There were other, single tables scattered around. I tried to count the chairs at ours but couldn't. They all merged together down at the far end. They were high-backed and hand-carved with red plush inserts. The snowy whiteness of the d'oilies and napkins and the brightness of the silverware made the dark wood of the table gleam as if it was black. The lights in the silver candlesticks down the table centre were shaped like real candles. They were all switched off except at the end of the main table where we were. There was a soft light from overhead. The walls were big panels of dark wood with paintings of noble people looking down at us. The floor was tiled like the foyer.

I made my first mistake going in. There was a man near the door doing something with some silver dishes at a sideboard. I thought he'd be a butler. He had white gloves on and was perfectly dressed. I didn't want to be rude and ignore him. So I said, 'Bon soir', meaning 'Good evening.' He paused long enough in what he was doing to give me one look. He took me in from head to feet and plainly said, 'Don't you try any tricks with me, young miss, or you won't stay here very long. You just watch yourself.' And he carried on with what he was doing.

The next was the dinner. They put me between the boys. I was glad. The girls were on the other side, and all the things down the middle would hide me if I made any mistakes. M'sieu was at the end; on the other side of Gilbertee.

What worried me was the row of knives and forks and things on each side. I didn't know what they were all for. There were so many of them.

I thought I'd be smart. I would watch M'sieu and do what he did. When he took a bit, I took a bit. When he said 'No, thanks', I said 'No, thanks.' And I watched and used the same things he used. It went along fine. I was awfully tempted. Some of the things he passed up on looked and smelled scrumptious, but I didn't risk it.

But then he put his napkin down and said, 'Yes. Well, you'll have to excuse me not eating much. But I daren't. I have to eat too much when I'm out. People get offended if I don't. But you go ahead and have whatever you want. I expect you can handle it better than I can. You've still got some growing to do.'

It was an awful letdown. I was still starving, and everything had gone. There was only the coffee.

He said it would be served in his bureau. But coffee doesn't agree with me. We never had it at home. So I asked to be excused. I wanted to do my unpacking. He said if he didn't see me at breakfast, he'd like to see me in his bureau around eleven.

I asked where I could get my overcoat and suitcase. He spoke to the butler about it. I thought he sounded sharp. The butler said he'd brought them in and they'd gone up. I said they hadn't been there when I came down. Their French was fast and I wasn't sure of some of it. He got awfully stiff. He said they'd probably been put in the wardrobe. I said I hadn't seen any wardrobe either. It was only Nicole who saved it. She said she'd come up and show me. But as I came out, I could feel Albert's eyes boring into the back of my head.

When we got up there, the bedspread was gone, and the bed had been turned back. And there was a wardrobe. It took up one entire wall from floor to ceiling. Nicole went and opened it. Two matching light-rosewood doors with silver handles met at a centre-post. Inside was a perfect cavern of hanging space. At each end was a wide bank of drawers. Hanging in the middle, in solitary splendour, was my beige coat on a hanger. Below it, on the floor, my suitcase, with its garish-looking rug, looked awful. I wondered whatever they'd thought.

Nicole must have thought they looked lonely because she asked if my other things would be coming later. I nearly said yes but realised it would've been fatal. There wouldn't be anything else coming later, and she'd find out in due course. Mother always said one fib had to be thatched with another, and the rain would always find its way through. To give myself time to think, I grabbed the suitcase and hefted it over to the chaise longue.

'Well, no, Nicole,' I said, working on the straps. 'This is all I brought. There won't be anything else. I was on my own, you see, and couldn't manage any more. Not with a shoulder bag. I only brought what I needed for now. I didn't know how long I'd be stopping. I didn't know if I was going to like it. And I didn't know if you were going to like me. Did I? It would've been silly bringing a whole lot of stuff and then having to take it all home again. And it's not safe to have things sent. Too much gets stolen. Anything else I want, I can get.'

It satisfied her, and she was quiet. I began taking things out and putting them in heaps for the different drawers.

'And is it zat you like us?' The wistfulness was there. 'Is it zat you will stay?'

'I can't say that, Nicole. It doesn't only depend on me. It depends on you people too. Of course I like you. You're all lovely. Especially Gilbertee. He's just adorable. But the thing is, do you like me? Do you want me to stay?"

'Oh, but yes. You are different. You are not like ze ozzers. Papa say zis time we must get someone different. And you are. You are nice.'

'Oh, but what are zey? Is it zat I can look? If you please?'

I'd picked up a pair of huggies. I gave them to her to look at. She let them unfold. She held them by the shoulders in front of herself and looked down over them. They were miles too big. They nearly reached her ankles.

'Oh!' she giggled. 'But what are zey? What do you call zem?'

'They're huggies. They're for underwear. Nothing else will keep you warm in Scotland. Mother makes them for us.'

She let out a squeal of laughter.

'Uggies! Uggies! Oh, but zey are fantastique!' Still holding them to her shoulders, she rushed to the door and out. I heard her going along the landing, calling out, 'Therese! Therese!' followed by a mad chatter of French.

The suitcase was empty, and I was on my second trip across to the wardrobe when they came back. They were in fits. Therese had the huggies.

'But what are zese?' she said.

'They're huggies. For underwear.'

'And is it zat you wear zem now, yes?'

'Yes, I am.' I undid the sleeve of my blouse and let them see where they came to my elbow. I lifted the hem of my skirt so they could see where they came to my knees.

'Oh, but zay are fantastique. Zey are, how you say, crazy, yes. You cannot wear zem here, in France. You will, how you say, boil? No. Cook! But yes. Zat is it. You will cook, no? It is too hot here.'

A sudden thought came to her. She looked at Nicole. A motion with her head, and they both went out, carefully shutting the door behind them.

I went on putting things away. Every drawer had a small cachet of lavender in it. They weren't away long.

'Is it zat you do not like our cooking?' Therese asked when they came back. They both watched me.

'Don't like the cooking, Therese? Why do you ask that? There was nothing wrong with the cooking. It was perfect. Why?'

'Zen is it zat you are on ze diet?'

'No. I'm not on a diet. But why? What's the trouble?'

'Zen, is it zat you have eaten on ze train or at Calais, yes?'

'No. I didn't have anything on the train. Nor at Calais either. I didn't have a thing since last night on the train from Scotland. I had some sandwiches Mother had given me. But why do you ask?"

'But zen why is it zat you eat nozzing? You say no to everysing and only have ze little bit. We see. Is it zat you are ill, yes? You are sick? Or is it zat you are too hot, oui?'

'Oh, is that what it is? Oh, that's nothing, Therese. Don't worry about me. I'll be all right. I'll catch up at breakfast.'

'Ah!' It was almost a chorus, as if they'd both suddenly understood something. With another look between them, they went off out again.

Nicole came back alone. Everything was put away and tidy, and I was on the chaise longue, revelling in it all and thinking of that gorgeous bath waiting for me. She said Therese was writing a letter and could she come and talk to me. I made room for her on the chaise longue.

I asked her about the other governesses. She said they'd had five. None of them were much good. The last one, Fifi, was from Paris. She'd taken Gilbertee into the park and left him there while she went off with a man she'd picked up. It was only luck they'd ever seen Gilbertee again. M'sieu had said he wouldn't have anybody else from an agency. He'd advertise for himself. He'd chosen the *London Times* because he'd thought he might get someone different. He'd been glad to get my answer from Scotland. He'd only advertised the once.

It was as though it was meant to be. Dr McKay and Mr Ogilvy had only looked a couple of times. If Fifi hadn't played up just when she did, and if the others hadn't made him so fed up, I'd never have known about it. I'd probably have been doing Father's books.

Marie-Louise knocked on the door and came in with a tray under a white cloth. She set it down on the dressing table.

'Come on, my little one,' she said in French, taking off the cloth. 'You come and sit here and eat this. We don't want people starving in our house. Nicole. You stay and make sure she eats every bit of it.' And she bustled away out again.

I didn't need Nicole to watch me. I was hungry. I sat up and tucked in. It was all the lovely things I'd missed. She'd even brought me sweets. In fact, there was a bit too much.

'It was good, yes?' Nicole said when I sat back and put down the napkin.

The look on her face made me do what I'd wanted to before. I got up and went over and gave her a good hug.

'Oh you're a lovely kid,' I told her. 'I bet that was your idea, wasn't it. Therese might have thought of it first but it was you that went and did it, wasn't it? Gosh you're lovely. No one's ever done anything like that for me before. My mother couldn't. Father'd never let her. Anyway, we never had nice things like that. You're a nice kid.'

'You're nice too,' she said and hugged me back. 'I hope you will stay.'

It made us sort of sisters. We could have been too. I was older and taller. My hair would have been longer than hers if I hadn't had it cut. And I wished I hadn't. It would have been just as thick and nice. It was black, and hers was nearly as gingery as Therese's. Her eyes were clear blue, and mine were dark brown. But that didn't matter. We needed each other. I needed a new family, and she needed someone to talk to. Therese was too busy with her love.

We went down together with the tray. She wanted to take it, but I said I had to find my way about. And I wanted to thank Marie-Louise myself. Marie-Louise was pleased too. Afterwards, we went back up to my room and talked. We talked till late.

She wanted to know all about Scotland. She was interested and asked questions. I told her about the charter parties with the Navy men. All the trips. And the things I'd seen. While they were fishing, I'd get a couple of big ones for us and then go off for a ramble. I found places where nobody had ever been before. I'd climb up and look over, and the mists would gradually thin. Everything would be fresh and new. Lovely colours would come up out of the ground. The palest of mauves and greens and blues. They'd float up and mingle together. Out in the middle, a fat trout would jump. *Plop!* The ripples would spread right out to the banks. As if it was the signal, a bright white finger would point down through the clouds. It would move slowly over the water until it came to a big rock. It would stay there and light it, like an altar. All around, there'd be things that looked like priests, or they could have been tall clumps of white heather. I could never be sure. Suddenly the light would go out. As if they knew they were being watched. The mists would come down again and hide it all. It didn't matter how long I waited it wouldn't go away. I'd only get soaked. Sometimes they'd send a blizzard, and I'd have to clamber down and run. We'd all have to get in the car and go home. I never told them why.

'But is it zat someone was really zere?'

'I could never be sure. And when I'd go back when the weather was clear, to find out, I'd never find the place again. It would be all changed. I went back on a motorbike one day by myself. I was sure I knew how to find the place. A blizzard chased me all the way home. I was lucky it didn't get me. I asked Mother about it, and she said I was fey. She was pleased, though.'

'What is fey?'

'It's a word we have. It means you can see things other people can't. Hidden things.'

'But were you not afraid? Alone wiz all zose men? How old were you?'

'I started when I was about eleven. But I wasn't afraid of them. They were lovely men. They were like big brothers and uncles. They always brought something for me for dinner. We have dinner in the middle of the day. We call it supper at night. I could have had wine too, but I never did. Mother said I shouldn't. And besides, I had to drive.'

'Oh, but wine does not hurt you. It is good. It does not hurt your driving. Papa often has it and drives.'

'Maybe yours is different. Anyway, Mother said I shouldn't, and so I never did. But they were lovely. Some of them were admirals and captains and commanders. Sometimes they didn't want to go shooting or fishing. They'd only want to get away from the sea. They'd have cameras, and I'd take them into the country. We'd all just sit and look. Sometimes they'd give me something for myself. My brother and I would go halves. We'd never tell Father. He'd want it.'

After she'd gone I soaked in my bath and then crawled into bed and snuggled. It was heavenly. I offered a little prayer of thanks to him for bringing me to it. And I blessed Fifi and the others for doing their bit.

*   *   *

ANNE ANGELO

CHAPTER 13

The House

I DIDN'T SEE ANYONE at breakfast. I dallied a bit before I went down after I heard the gong but there was nobody around. Everything was there on the sideboard, so I helped myself. Then I went for a wander.

It was huge. The ground floor was all living area. The hallway the housekeeper had come out of went from the foyer in the front through to a wide tiled patio at the back. Opening off the hallway were the dining room, the large and small drawing rooms, the butler's pantry, a servery for bringing the food up from the kitchens, a room for the housekeeper and for the ironing, a flight of stairs going down to the basement and kitchens and laundries, and a flight of stairs going up at the back to the top floor for the servants.

The tiled patio at the back had ornate iron railings and went the full width of the house. Ten marble steps went down from it to the driveway and the gardens.

The French windows opened right out so guests could go from one to the other and mingle. Each of the drawing rooms had a grand piano. There was no dark panelling as in the dining room. They were brighter and with no paintings staring down.

The driveway went right round inside the walls. There were streets on three sides; four counting Rue Nationale out at the front. The walls were high and brick with a car entrance in the middle. You could drive right in, round and out again. The centre was all lawns and flowerbeds, shrubs and pools, stone gnomes, animals, and bird baths. It was all in perfect order. I saw three gardeners.

The house was built around the foyer. M'sieu's bureau and rooms, as I said, were halfway up to the first floor and looked out over the back. But from his door he could see down across the foyer to the front door. The first floor was suites for the family and guests. They were all different. There was a Blue Room, a Green Room, my Louis the XIV, a Gold Room, and so on. They were all complete with their own bathrooms and everything. The top floor was the servants' quarters and storerooms for linen and things. I saw two maids and caught a glimpse of Marie-Louise and the butler.

Around eleven, I knocked on the bureau door. I'd put on my second-best costume. It was mid-green, and I had a cream-yellow blouse. He was pleased to see me.

'Ah, that's nice,' he said. 'Not quite so Scottish, eh? And you're right on time. I like that. I like people to be punctual. All right, well do come in. Well now. What did we have? Oh yes. Your French.'

He went to a bookshelf and took a book. He opened it at random and gave it to me with his thumb marking the place.

'Here,' he said. 'Read this to me.'

It was Dumas in French.

'Yes,' he said after a very short while. 'Well, you'll have to polish up on that, won't you?'

He gave me a French-English dictionary and a book of French poems.

'Keep these by your bed. If you read for an hour or so every night before going to sleep, you'll find you'll improve in no time. The subconscious works on it while you're sleeping. Any word you don't know, look it up on the spot. Learn one new word every day, and you'll be surprised. The rhyme in the poems will help you with the pronunciation. Good. So that's that. Now, what else? Oh yes. Your religion. I suppose you are Christian, are you?'

'Christian? Why, yes, of course. My father's an elder of the Presbyterian Church. I used to be leader of our Sunday school group. But I'm afraid I lost interest. My brother and I stopped going to church. We didn't like some of the things they said and did. But if you want me to take the children to church, I don't mind.'

'No, no. It wasn't that. It was just something Nicole told me. It made me wonder if maybe you were pagan or something. So that's fine, then. Now what else was there? I think that's about all. There was your driving, but that can wait. So now it's your turn.

'What do you think of us? Do you think you're going to like it here? I know I'm not giving you much time, but I haven't got much time to give you. I told you I have to be away a lot. I do. I have to be away again this afternoon. Now you've met the children and you've had a look round the house. What do you think? You seem to have got on well with everybody. Albert, of course? Well, I think he'll come round all right in time. He's a good man, but he's had rather a rough time from some of the others. Don't rush him. Now what do you think?'

I told him I liked it already. My room was a dream. The girls were nice, and the housekeeper was a dear. She was like my own mother. The trouble with the butler could have been my own fault. I shouldn't have spoken to him. And I hadn't noticed the wardrobe. I asked him what sort of hours I'd have to keep with the teaching and what I should do if anyone was naughty.

He smiled.

'I don't think you'll find any of them very naughty,' he said. 'Gilbertee might be sometimes, but I think you'll be able to handle him easy enough. The teaching isn't the important thing. You've probably noticed their English is fairly good now. It'll improve with you here, of course. But the main thing is to have someone here I can rely on to keep an eye on them while I'm away. It's too much for the housekeeper. She has enough to do with the house. It needs someone like yourself who's young enough to be on their level but old enough to keep control. I think you could do it very well.

'Gilbertee's my main concern. The others will be away at their schools most of the time. They'll be going off on Monday. Then you'll only have him. That'll be your job. Making sure he's looked after and happy. And there'll be the odd message for the housekeeper. She's in charge when I'm not here.

'Now how does that sound to you? If there's anything you don't like, say so and we'll try and sort it out. Or if you don't think it's going to suit you, tell me now, and I can make other arrangements. But don't fool me about. I don't want to have to come back because something's gone wrong. Be honest with me.'

'I don't see anything can go wrong,' I said. 'I think I will be happy here. You've all been marvellous to me so far. Nicole and Therese are almost like sisters. I'll look after Gilbertee for you. At any rate, I promise you I won't go and leave him in the park.'

It made him smile again.

'So they told you about that, did they? Yes, well that just simply wasn't good enough. We can't have any more of that. All right, then. So that's that."

He held out his hand, and we shook hands on it.

'So it's a deal, then. And I can assure you, Anne, if you keep your end of it, you won't be sorry. I assure you of that. Now what else was there? Oh yes. Your clothes. Now I don't want you to misunderstand me. There's nothing wrong with your clothes. They're very nice. But I don't think they're quite suitable. They're too hot, for one thing. Our summers here get very warm. The girls are quite concerned for you. And apart from that, it's a matter of style. We want you to be like one of the family. You'll be meeting people, here and elsewhere. You'll have to represent the family. And you can't do it if you're dressed like—well, like Bonnie Prince Charlie, for example. Can you?'

He smiled, and I knew what he meant. I told him I'd already realised it myself. I'd been uncomfortable ever since I got off the boat at Calais. I'd do something about it as soon as I could.

'Good. So that's no problem either. I'd suggest you put yourself in the girls' hands. They've got something in mind for you. Nicole especially. She's got excellent taste in such matters. Be advised by her. She has a gift for it.

'So now there's only your driving. How good are you? Do you think you could take me into the city? There'll be some parking, and it can get hectic. What do you think? Can you handle it, or should we leave it till some other time?"

'I don't care. I don't see it'll be all that different. I've driven most sorts. We have fifteen, and they're all different models. I've never scraped nor bumped one yet.' And I hadn't. Except the time Father fiddled with the brakes and I ended up in the burn. I didn't tell him about that, though.

'All right,' he said. 'Run those up to your room. By the time you get back I'll be ready for you.'

The garage was on the other side of the side street. We went out the front onto Rue Nationale and turned left. We turned left again into the Rue Solferino. Seeing our brick wall from outside, it was even more like a fortress. It was at least eight feet high and had jagged bits of broken glass set in the top. The garage was across on the other side. It looked as if it'd been a warehouse. There were three cars in it. The Buick, a late-model Chevrolet, and a Lancia—a Lambda model the same as father's latest. There was a forty-four-gallon drum of benzene with a hand pump lying on top of it. And there was a pit in the floor for getting down to do repairs.

He asked if I could get the Chevy out. I said I could. It'd been driven in and was a bit squeezy, but I managed it. It was the first left-hand drive I'd driven. He made me take him round the back and in through the gates. Round the drive and out again. And then round to the front onto Rue Nationale and into Lille. I soon got used to it. Parking was a bit tricky with the left-hand drive, but I was careful. Then it was back home again. He was pleased.

'Oh yes,' he said. 'You'll do.'

I backed it in. He asked me why. So I told him.

'It's easier. You've either got to back out with a cold motor or else back in with a hot one. You've got to have it one way or the other. It's easier with a hot motor. Most of our drivers were Navy men. We hired our cars out. And some of them weren't very good drivers. So we had to make it as easy as we could. Our hangar wasn't very big. We only had a few inches between them. My father would've had a fit if we'd scraped one. They were his pride and joy.'

'Well, well. That's something new. I've never heard of that before. You're quite surprising, aren't you? It's a good idea. You can keep those keys in your purse. Use the Chevy anytime you want. If you need benzene or anything done, see Jacques. He'll fix it for you.'

It was lovely. Father would never have said a thing like that. The best I ever got out of him was a grunt. No matter how well I'd done something. Most times, it was a grouch because I hadn't done it better. Peter and I'd often wondered if there was something wrong with us, the way father was. And the way the other kids treated us because we were 'foreigners'. These people thought I was all right. They must do to treat me as they did. I hadn't been here for a full day yet, and I'd got the keys of the car. They'd all taken to me, and I hadn't really done anything to make them. I'd only been myself.

He got away that afternoon. He was going to Brussels and Liege. He thought he'd be away for about a week. Anything I wanted, I was to go to Marie-Louise.

I soon found out what the girls had in mind for me. They wanted me to take them into Lille shopping the next morning. Marie-Louise said it would be better in the afternoon. Gilbertee would be down for his nap then. She would put one of the maids to keep an eye on him. I would be free.

I'd never seen such a mad spending of money. Father would have had a fit. It didn't mean a thing to them. If they saw something they wanted, they took it and signed for it. It was all on account. They were known in all the stores. I stood back. Their French was too fast. I didn't want to risk getting dragged in and not understanding and making a fool of myself. I saw the saleswomen looking at me and talking, but I thought they were asking, was I with them. It wasn't until we got home that I learned the truth. By that time, the back of the Chevy was piled high with boxes and packets of all descriptions. I thought I was only the carrier and driver.

The whole lot was taken up to my room and piled on my bed. And then it started. It was the maddest session. Three crazy females giggling and opening things and tossing the wrappers and boxes onto the floor. I had to go and take off my huggies and my hand-knitted stockings and try everything on. It wasn't in the least embarrassing. We were like three sisters.

There were gorgeous silk things I'd never dreamed of. I found out why they were both so well developed. I was more so. When I first looked in the mirror and saw the effect that brassiere and those lovely silk underthings had, I was horrified. What had been a couple of shapeless lumps on my chest was now wicked. Absolutely wicked. If Mother had seen me, she'd have made me 'go and take that thing off this instant! Go on, you shameless hussy!' My legs looked different altogether. The sheer silk of the stockings and the style of the shoes made them look terrific. The girdles had little tabs to clip the stockings on, and as I fixed them, I knew garters and hand-knitted stockings were things of the past. These new things looked and felt so delicious. I was emerging from my shabby old chrysalis. The world was wonderful.

They hadn't bought just one each of them. They'd got them by the half-dozens. There were day frocks and evening dresses. There was one peach of a gown in slinky black. It had a high neck with white lace at the throat and rows of little white buttons holding the wrists close. I felt like a duchess. Everything fitted. Their judgement had been marvellous. But Nicole was maddening. They'd got me large squares of coloured silks for headwear. She could take one and, with a simple twist of her wrist, make it look ravishing. When I tried it, no matter what I did, it only looked like some frump making out she was a nursing sister. I hated to think what M'sieu would say when he saw the bills. It must have cost a fortune.

Going down for dinner, I had a final look in the mirror. I was a new me, stepping into a new world. Scotland was gone forever. That door had shut. Nobody would ever think I was Bonnie Prince Charlie again. I blessed those two girls and everybody else in 241.

*   *   *

CHAPTER 14

Relations

MOTHER HAD OFTEN told us, 'When one door closes, another opens.' One opened like a miracle to me now into a world I'd never dreamed I'd see. It allowed me to enter that world of wealth, comfort, and kindness she'd known before things went wrong. It was as if a wheel had gone full circle, returning me to where I'd started. I was like the salmon and trout that go back to their spawning grounds. It might have been only circumstance that took me there, but it was her hand that did it. She'd always taught us 'When you're right, stick to your guns, no matter who's against you or how black things seem.' And that's all I did. But it turned out marvellously. It couldn't have happened any other way.

The following Monday, I took the three older ones to their trains to go back to their schools. When I got home, there'd been a phone call. Marie-Louise said I had to take Gilbertee round to his bonne-maman's, his grandmother's. She was a Madame Crecy who lived in the Rue de Turenne about three kilometres away. I had to go west along Rue Nationale away from the city and turn right into Rue de Turenne towards the canal. She was M'sieu's mother-in-law. She would expect me after lunch.

I had no trouble finding the house. Its tall wrought-iron fence made it stand out. The house sat back nearly hidden by trees and shrubs. The driveway circled a perfectly kept lawn, which had the little white hoops they use in croquet sticking up here and there. The gates were open, so I drove in and parked just clear of the front door. Shrubs and flowerbeds pressed hard against the outside edge of the drive.

A maid came out and took us into a drawing room. It was a little bigger than our small one, but much more airy and bright, more feminine. The furniture was Jacobean, and the decor grey floral with floor-to-ceiling curtains all in pastel shades.

Madame Crecy was tall and angular and aristocratic. She walked with a walking stick with a big silver knob. Her hair was pulled back tightly into a bun like my mother's. She had a large bony nose, prominent cheekbones, and a high forehead. A pair of pince-nez hung by a fine gold chain from the front of her dress. She went past me to the window and turned to survey me from there. The light was in my face.

'So you're the new girl, are you?' she said. It wasn't friendly. It was even hostile. Her eyes were sharp and watchful.

'I'm the new governess, madame, if that's what you mean', I said. I didn't see why I shouldn't. It was what I was. 'I was asked to bring Gilbertee here. Here he is.'

I had him by the hand, wondering what she wanted us for.

'New governess, are you? Hmm!' It was nearly a sneer. 'That's a fine-sounding position. I wonder if you're capable of filling it.'

She came close and held her pince-nez up to her eyes and peered at me through them. I felt like something under a microscope.

Her face wasn't really sour. The mouth was firm but well-shaped and not down at the corners. I wondered if she was having a bad day.

'Hmm!' she snorted when she'd seen enough. 'You don't look so very different to me. I don't see any Bonnie Prince Charlie. You look just like all the others, and I expect you are. However, we'll soon find out. Have you got permission to drive that Chevrolet?'

'Yes I have.' I didn't say any more. It wasn't any of her business. If she wanted to be like this, she could. But I didn't have to take any rubbish from her. I'd been told to bring Gilbertee to her. I'd done it. If she wanted to be nasty, I'd take him away again just as quickly. She meant nothing to me.

She went back to her window and tugged on a bell cord. And then stood looking out with her back to me.

A maid came.

'Ah yes, Charmian,' Madame said. She came and took Gilbertee's other hand and walked him across to her. 'Here', she said. 'Take this young fellow and attend to him please.'

The maid took him and went out, closing the door. It was done before I could stop them. But I didn't like it. He didn't need any attending to. He was long past that stage. And anyway, if he did, it was my job. I could attend to anything he wanted. It was what I was being paid for. I didn't like it one little bit, but I didn't say anything because after all, she was his grandmother.

'There,' she said, going back to her window. 'That deals with that, doesn't it?' She rested both hands on her stick and leaned on them, facing me. 'Now you're free. You can go and do whatever you like. You've got nothing to worry about.'

She was pleased. As if she'd solved some problem. But I didn't understand.

'How do you mean? I'm free?'

'Well, you are. You're free to go off and do whatever you want. I expect your young man's waiting for you somewhere. You can go off with him and do anything you like. We won't need you now until your master gets back. We'll look after Gilbertee.'

She tugged again on her bell cord.

'But I don't want to go anywhere, madame. I haven't got a young man. and if I had, I wouldn't be going off with him. My place is here with Gilbertee. And if you don't mind, please, I'd like to have him now. It's nearly time for his afternoon nap. I'd like to be getting him home.'

'Oh no. You haven't got to worry about that. We'll see he has his nap. We'll look after him now. But you can go.'

A maid came: it was a different one.

'Yes, Julie,' Madame said. 'This young person's leaving. Show her out, will you, please? Good afternoon, mam'selle.'

I still didn't understand. Not until I looked at them and saw the look they gave each other. They both looked smug. And they both watched me. Suddenly I understood. I went hot and cold as I realised what I'd done. I'd thrown everything away. M'sieu would never forgive me. The very first time out, and I'd let someone take him away from me. I didn't know what things were like between him and his mother-in-law.

ANNE ANGELO

It could cost me my job. I'd have nowhere to go. I hadn't any money, and I couldn't go back to Invergordon. I might even have to pay for all the new clothes. I'd never be able to find him. They could shift him from room to room. They could even have got him out of the house. I was near tears as I thought of it. I thought they were the two most hateful people I'd ever met. And then I thought of the police. There was a station not far from us in Rue Nationale. I'd go to them: they'd help me.

'All right, madame,' I said. 'You can do that. You can have me put out if you want to. But I warn you. If you do, I'll go straight round to the police. There's a station in Rue Nationale. I'll have you charged with kidnapping and abduction. He's in my care, and you've taken him from me. I don't know what you're trying to do, but you're not getting away with it.'

It surprised them both. It was in their faces. They looked at each other and back at me. Madame put on her glasses again and came and studied me.

'Well, well,' she said at last. 'So you'd do that, would you? You'd go to the Gendarmerie? Well, well. What do you think of that, Julie? And I really believe she would too. What are we going to do with her? She really is different, isn't she?'

'All right, Julie,' she said after a while. 'You can go. If I need you again, I'll ring.'

'Well now,' she said when the maid had gone and we were alone. 'What are we going to do about this? Suppose we sit down and have a little chat? We could have some afternoon tea? Or maybe you'd prefer coffee? I think we've got things to talk about.'

'No, thank you, madame. I don't want to sit down and talk. And I don't want any afternoon tea, thank you very much. I only want to take Gilbertee and go home. It's past his time, and he'll be getting tired."

'Yes, of course,' she said. 'You're all annoyed and upset, aren't you? You think I'm a horrible old woman who's tricked you. But I assure you, it's not what you think. It's for a very good purpose. We're as concerned about him as you are.'

She was silent, thinking.

'How would it be', she said, 'if I took you to see him? So you could see for yourself he's all right? Would you like that? He's probably asleep by now, but if we're quiet, we shouldn't disturb him. What do you say? Would it make you feel any better?'

'Yes, it would,' I said. I'd grab him and get him out of there somehow or other, and they'd never get him away from me again. They could go to pot.

She led the way, and I was glad. If she'd called a maid, it would have meant I had someone else to deal with. It was better with just her. I knew I could find the front door.

She stopped at a door on the first floor and put her finger on her lips to shush me. Then she opened it quietly and peeped in. She pushed it wider and let go the handle so I could get past.

He was asleep in a bed. He looked so lovely no one could've disturbed him. He was on his side with one arm round a big ginger teddy just like his own one at home. Bright gold curls were spread on the pillow. There was a box of toys on the floor, and a small bike leaned against the dressing table. His clothes were folded neatly on a chair. It was a nice airy room. The blind was nearly down, but the window was open. The curtains moved gently.

She tapped me on the shoulder. She was different altogether. She was smiling. Her face was all soft and happy. Her eyes were quite dewy. She beckoned me out. I looked back at him. I didn't know what it was all about, but I did know one thing. Somebody here loved him. They didn't mean him any harm. I followed her out.

'Oh my dear,' she said softly when the door was closed. 'Isn't he the loveliest little fellow?' She looked close into my face and then took my arm. 'Come on,' she said. 'Let's go down and have some afternoon tea. I need some, and I expect you do too. Come along. He'll be all right where he is.'

We'd had our afternoon tea, and the things had been taken away. We sat and talked. She asked me about Invergordon. I told her about Mother and Peter and everything. She was interested.

'Well now', she said, 'about Gilbertee. What are we going to do about him? I know you're looking after him, and I don't doubt you're going to do it properly. But things have happened, and we don't want them to happen again. I've been thinking. How would it be if you moved in here with us? There's a room up there alongside his. Say, until your master gets back? You'd be free to come and go as you liked. That way we'd both be sure he was safe, wouldn't we? I think you'd find it better here than at 241. There's nothing much there now the children are away. What do you think? If Marie-Louise wants you, she can ring.'

I didn't know what to think. I went up and had a look at the room. Julie took me. She was different too. She was quite nice. It wasn't like my Louis the Fourteenth, but it was comfortable. It was a nice house. It didn't have the tiling we had. There were more soft carpets and wallpapers. And there was no wide sweeping staircase.

I asked if I could use the phone. I rang Marie-Louise. She was pleased.

'Oh, but yes, my little one! But of a certainty! If Bonne-maman wants you to do that, you do it. It will be all right with M'sieu. And listen, ma petite. You be nice to Bonne-maman. She is very wealthy, and if she likes you like that, you are very lucky. She can do much for you. I will ring if I want you. Bon chance, ma petite!'

And it was good luck. It was the best luck I've ever had in my whole life. It was through Bonne-maman taking to me like that that made possible all the things that happened to me later. She opened a door for me. Through her I mingled and was accepted by the crème de la crème of French society. I met them as an equal. I ceased to be a governess. I became her protege.

She'd lost her daughter, the children's mother, from leukaemia three years earlier. Within a year of that loss, her husband had died. She'd been desperately lonely. She'd put all her love into Gilbertee. The stupid governesses they'd had, had almost driven her mad. I was what she'd been wanting. She took me everywhere with her.

She had everybody to her house for dinner on Fridays. They were a big family and very wealthy. They had linen mills at Marcq on the way to Turcoing towards the Belgian border. They were a widespread family, but they all came: husbands and wives, children and their governesses. It was her way of bringing them together and keeping an eye on them.

I didn't have my meals with the other governesses. I wasn't one any longer. I was family.

I was always home when M'sieu was. And I was always there when the children were home from their schools. But nearly all the rest of my time was spent with Bonne-maman. We went everywhere. We'd go out into the country visiting the members of the family and stay for days. They were all refined, cultured, well-educated people. I absorbed their ways. My French became even better than theirs. I could quote poetry few of them had ever read. It's often that way with foreigners. They learn a language better than those it belongs to. I became as thoroughly haute bourgeoisie as my mother. The wheel had completed its circle.

I even pitied my mother. That she could have been so foolish as to have thrown all this away. But I was to realise that I was her daughter. Part of her was in me. Her dangers were my dangers. I'd have been in a far worse mess if a watchful hand hadn't stopped me. There was no credit due to me.

*   *   *

ANNE ANGELO

CHAPTER 15

Switzerland

IT WAS ONLY a few months later, in November of 1934, that Bonne-maman opened that door wider. It was as if she'd decided I'd acquired enough polish. It was time I got on with other things. She kept a maternal eye on all of us. I was twenty-one. There should be some male interest in my life. She took me to Switzerland for the Winter Sports, where she knew there'd be hordes of wealthy young men. All the eligible men in our circle were already earmarked for members of the family. She bought me a stunning ski outfit guaranteed to make a prisoner of any male who saw me in it. She thought to turn me loose in it up on the snow slopes, and Nature would take its course. Nature did. But it wasn't quite in the way she'd intended. I hadn't told her my mother's history. You don't talk about things like that. So she didn't know what was hidden in my nature. She didn't know either of my abysmal ignorance of men and their ways. It was only her own quick perceptions and knowledge of the world that saved the day. Those ski clothes were most effective. Cupid rubbed his hands with glee when she bought them.

It was at one of her Friday dinners late in October that she made the announcement. Out of the blue, she said she was going to take the waters at Evian-les-Bains. Gilbertee and I would go with her. We would go on up to the snow fields and learn to ski. It would do us both good. We'd be away for a fortnight. She'd arrange for instructors and buy me the proper clothes. It was fabulous.

M'sieu agreed but said we'd have to be back before the other children got home from their end-of-year term. He'd be away in Belgium. Otherwise, it would work in very well. And so it was arranged.

If I'd known her real reason, I doubt I'd have gone. I wouldn't have wanted anything to do with men, although I'd certainly have been attracted by the skiing. Toshack and Geordie McPhail and Father's schemes for me had been plenty. I hadn't forgotten the way he ordered Mother upstairs and into bed when she'd wanted to go to her dying mother. I wasn't going to give any man that sort of power over me.

My world was perfect as it was. I didn't want anything to change. Everything I could possibly want was provided for me. I had no potatoes to dig, no flowers and whisky to sell to get myself pocket money, no father demanding nearly all my wages. I banked half and sent the other half home to Mother. I knew she got it. I sent it through Dr McKay.

I'd realised what a horror her life must be. I'd been reared in that life. I'd never known any better. Suddenly I'd been released and found this paradise. For her it was the opposite. This was the life she'd known. Suddenly she'd been snatched away and taken into that. In place of this lovely warm climate, wealth and affection, she had freezing blizzards, deprivation, and hatred. For her there'd be no release, no reprieve. Her letters showed her utter hopelessness. Dr McKay could do no more for her. Her diabetes was getting steadily worse. He said it was as much the misery and isolation as the poor food. The cure was in her own hands. But we knew she would never take it.

The morning we set out for Switzerland is as fresh in my mind as yesterday. It was clear, fresh, and bracing. Autumn was well on its way. Bonne-maman's big opulent Packard was packed and ready to go. They had trouble getting all our suitcases into the boot. Mother's, with its Stewart rug strapped to its side, wasn't among them. It was put away in the back of my wardrobe, along with my Stewart costume and Glengarry. The Scottish tawpie who'd been so proud of them was gone. Bonne-maman had got me everything new. I didn't know it then, but I was the picture of the modern young French female. My ski instructor told me. He taught me lots of things.

The three of us sat together in the back seat: Bonne-maman looking every inch the wealthy aristocrat, Gilbertee in the middle looking the perfect golden-haired cherub, and me in the other corner. Gustave, her dignified Swedish chauffeur, firmly closed the door, and with his shiny

ANNE ANGELO

peaked cap at precisely the correct angle and his blue uniform spotless, climbed into the front and started up. They all waved and wished us 'Bon voyage' and 'Bon chance'. We rolled round the drive, out, and away.

We stopped at Cambrai for lunch. It was at Cambrai I saw my first real parasols. They were in the window of the little boutique next door. They were so dainty and feminine they instantly reminded me of the one Mother had made for me. Bonne-maman bought them both and left them there to be picked up on our way back. She said I had to take them while I could. There weren't many of them about. One had a curved handle like a small umbrella. The other was straight and carved just like that first one. They were so exquisite I began collecting them. My collection was to save me from a nightmare far worse than Toshack could have been.

We got to Reims for our first night. She had friends there. We didn't get in until late, so I didn't see much of the city. In the morning, we got away early and reached St Dizier for lunch and Dijon for the night. Her friends there had a big estate and a beautiful chalet. From Dijon we drove on through Chalon to Tournus for lunch, Gustave was a steady driver. If Peter and I'd had that gorgeous Packard on those roads, we'd have done it in half the time. Bonne-maman didn't worry. She liked to tootle along enjoying the scenery. It was beautiful. All the trees were in their autumn clothes. We pressed on through Lyon to Chamberry for our third night. They had a party organised for us. Bonne-maman knew everybody. We had an easy run the next day through Geneva to Thonon-les-Bains and got to Evian-les-Bains early.

Bonne-maman stayed there with the car. She wanted to get started on her cure. The waters are supposed to be very good for the liver. Not that there was really anything wrong with Bonne-maman's liver. She was remarkably healthy. She must have been at least fifty-five or sixty and could do anything she wanted to. I think even her walking stick was only for effect.

Gilbertee and I caught the little paddle steamer across Lac Leman to Lausanne. She'd had us all booked into the Hotel Splendide. They drove round the lake, and we met again in the lounge waiting for dinner. After breakfast on Wednesday morning, I put on my ski things for the first time and looked at myself in the mirror. I told Bonne-maman I couldn't go out like that. Not in front of men. I'd have to wear a skirt as well. It was too revealing. She said I was being silly.

'You can't wear a skirt with that, my dear,' she said. 'You'd look ridiculous. In the first ten yards, it would be up round your shoulders. You'd only draw more attention to yourself. There's nothing wrong with you.'

'But I've never even worn pants before. And look at this pullover. It's far too tight. I look awful.'

'Of course you don't. There's nothing wrong with you. You've got a very nice figure. I tell you, my dear, if I were a young man, I'd very soon be wanting to know who you were. Now go on. Out you go and enjoy yourself. Look after Gilbertee, and I'll see you at dinner. Go on. Don't be bashful. No one will have any better. They're the latest style and the best quality I could find. Bye-bye now.'

But they did stare at me. Even the women did. I put on my goggles so they wouldn't know who I was and took Gilbertee by the hand. I saw the instructor have a second look as I came closer. But I didn't mind him. He was nice.

He was exactly what a ski instructor ought to be. He looked like a Viking. As if he'd been born and bred in the mountains. His name was Bjorgsen. He was tall and fair and rugged. He was either Norwegian or Danish. He had a lovely accent. And he knew everything there was to know about skiing.

He did Gilbertee first, and Gilbertee took to him straight away. He thought he was fun. Then he came to me.

The first thing he taught me was that modesty is a lot of rubbish. There's no such thing. There's no difference between men and women. If you want to learn to ski, you have to be taught. And that means taught. Talking wouldn't do it. You had to be shown. He was there to show me. That's what he was paid for.

He was a perfectionist. My feet had to be just so—so far apart and bent just so at the ankles. He said I had good ankles. Most people's were stiff. It was hopeless trying to ski with stiff ankles. My ankles

ANNE ANGELO

went where he put them. It was the same with my knees. I had good knees: they were nice and flexible. They had to be just so and over the feet. The legs had to be like coiled springs, ready for anything. He was surprised my hips were so stiff. He asked if I was self-conscious because I was wearing ski pants. Had I ever worn pants before? I told him I hadn't and I wasn't self-conscious. But I was. I was conscious of those warm hands gripping me. He held me all the time he was talking. My hips had to go farther forward, down a bit more, forward a bit farther. Couldn't I crouch better than that? It seemed odd. I had such good knees and ankles.

He stood to the side and looked from there.

'Oh yes. That's a bit better. You've got to do better than that, though. Now let's fix this back of yours.'

He put a hand on my back and the other on my front and simply bent me. It took my breath away. No one had ever put a hand on me there before. He must have known. The pullover didn't leave much room for doubt. I'm not flat chested. I don't need any padding. But it made no difference. He held me until I'd got the position he wanted. I turned my head to look at him. His face was near mine.

'No, no. Don't look at me,' he said. 'I don't want you to move. What do you think I'm going to all this trouble for? I want you to keep this position. I want you to practise it until it comes naturally.'

He put my head where he wanted it—looking straight ahead but not stiff.

'All right', he said, 'hold that and we'll take a run. Now don't be scared. Relax. I'll be right here behind you holding you so you don't fall. If you get tense, we'll both likely take a spill. Now you push off. Only use your arms, not your body.'

And away we went. It was terrific. He had me by the waist. Bonne-maman had been right. If I'd been wearing a skirt, it would have been up round my head in the first few yards.

He said I had good balance. If I wanted to, I could be very good. He said to go to him anytime I had a problem.

'That's what I'm here for,' he said. 'You've got to get the style right first. Speed and technique will come later. Work on those hips of yours. They're going to be your trouble.'

I did go back to him. I was intrigued. I couldn't see how he could be so entirely unconscious of me. I wanted him to put his hands on me again and then make him conscious of what he was doing. But I couldn't. He was like an artist with a model. He'd had so many pupils; I was just another one. I was just so much cheese. But I must have got through to him a bit because I got lots more time than the others did. He caught up to me as I was going in for lunch and asked me my other name. I told him it was Anne, but he said he'd call me Anna. He liked it better. He said his name was Hans. He was friendly. I walked on air.

I saw Gilbertee come a nasty cropper in the afternoon and went down. But by the time I got there, Hans already had him. I saw how strong he was. He picked him up with one hand and held him while he dusted him off. Gilbertee was spluttering and rubbing the snow out of his eyes and nose.

'That's not the way to do it,' Hans said to him. 'You're supposed to ski on your feet, not on your nose. It doesn't hurt so much. How are you? Are you all right?'

Gilbertee decided not to cry and laughed.

'That's better.' Hans set him down on his feet and gave him a push. 'Go on. Off you go. And stay on your feet. Crouch down more, and you won't fall so easy. Nice kid,' he said to me. 'I thought we were going to have tears then. But you must have been married very young, weren't you? He must be at least six or seven.'

'He's five,' I said. 'And I'm not married. I never have been.'

'Oh gee, I'm sorry,' he said. 'I mean, I didn't know. Look, I'm very sorry. It's none of my business. I shouldn't have opened my big mouth.'

'It's all right. You didn't say anything wrong,' I told him. 'It's just that he's not my child. I'm only looking after him for a friend. Are you married?'

'Me? Married? Gee, what an idea. Do I look like that, do I? Well, doesn't that show you? And here was I thinking I was looking especially good today. Oh well, never mind. That's the way it goes. Now what's

ANNE ANGELO

your problem this time? Still those hips of yours? You're still very stiff. I noticed you a while ago.'

'No, thanks. I'm all right this time. I only came down because I saw Gilbertee fall. I'm doing fine.'

And I was too. And I was doing better now I'd found that out. I was pleased. I hadn't thought he could be. He was too clean and nice. And he didn't know enough about women. I wondered if he even had a girlfriend.

It was the most thrilling day of my whole life. I'd stopped, up at the top, for a rest. It was a fantastic scene. It was clean and fresh and breathlessly exciting. I was in Europe's most fashionable winter resort, rubbing shoulders with all the wealthiest people, staying at the most exclusive hotel—learning to ski from the best instructor and wearing the most expensive and stylish skiing clothes that money could buy. It was only a few short months ago, in June, I hadn't had anything. I'd been scared for my life wondering who Father was going to put on to me next. It was almost unbelievable.

In the lounge that night, the three of us were waiting for dinner. Gilbertee was still excited. He was chattering away, telling Bonne-maman about the spills he'd had.

'Just listen to him, my dear,' she said proudly. 'What a day he's had.' She patted my hand. 'It's all your doing, you know, bless you. You're just what he's needed. You're like his own mother would've been. I couldn't do it. I'm far too old. It's a pity you two couldn't have met. You'd have had so much in common. She was a lovely girl. Well now. And how was the instructor?'

'He's nice,' Gilbertee chipped in. 'I like him. He's awful strong. He can pick me up one hand. Anne likes him too. Don't you, Anne? She says he's like a Viking.'

'Like a Viking, is he?' I saw her quick look at me and couldn't stop myself colouring up. It sounded so silly. 'Well now,' she said. 'We'll have to watch that, won't we? Vikings are very cruel men. They do nasty things to people. We don't want anything like that, do we?'

'No,' he said, suddenly all serious and round-eyed.

'He's not really like that, Bonne-maman,' I said. 'It's just that he's so tall and fair and rugged. And he's a marvellous instructor. He knows everything there is to know about skiing. He says I've got good balance and learn quickly. I could be very good if I wanted to.'

'Yes, my dear. You do have good balance. I've noticed that. And you do learn quickly. So that's fine. then. You'll both be all right again tomorrow. We'll be away early. And you be careful, young Gilbertee. Not too many spills. I don't want either of you getting hurt. Ah, there's the gong. Come along then.'

There was dancing and entertainment in the evening, but we didn't go. She was too tired, and I didn't feel like being in a crowd. I wanted to be alone to think over that wonderful day. And that's where Nature first took a hand.

When I'd been brushing up on my French, M'sieu had told me to do my study last thing at night before I went to sleep. He said my subconscious would work on it while I slept and I'd make better progress. It worked the same with skiing. My subconscious worked on it and came up with an idea I'd never have got otherwise. If I'd gone downstairs, I'd probably have dreamed of someone in the dance band.

I dreamed about Hans. We were by ourselves up on the top, and he asked me to marry him. He'd been working on my hips from behind. He came closer and brought his hands up onto my chest and caressed me. He said I was driving him crazy. He couldn't live without me. Would I marry him? I told him I would. It was so real it woke me up. I could still feel his hands fondling me. I put mine up where his had been and told myself they were his.

Suddenly there in the dark, it burst on me. I was in love with him! I wanted him as my man! I'd never thought of anyone like that before. But now it came to me. I needed someone. I needed someone to belong to, someone who'd belong to me. For always. I couldn't go on like this for the rest of my life. Gilbertee and the others would grow up. I wouldn't always have Bonne-maman. I'd be on my own. I needed someone. And I'd never find anyone better than Hans. He was everything I wanted.

He was good-looking. It was a good strong face: the sort of face I'd like to see in my children. He was strong and tall and broad-shouldered.

ANNE ANGELO

He had good eyes. They were deep blue. It was a good mouth. It wasn't afraid to smile. Gilbertee liked him. Children could tell. Our ages were right. I was twenty-one, he was about twenty-five. He had a good job. He'd be well paid. I could learn and become his assistant. We'd be a team. My languages would be useful. The future would be wonderful.

Something else my mother had said came to my mind. She'd told me I'd have to be careful with men when my time was right. She'd said everything would urge me on. It was Nature's way of making sure there'd be babies. My heart would play tricks on me. Hers had. I had to laugh to myself. My time was right now. It would be for the rest of the week. Maybe that's why this crazy idea had come to me. Everything had just fallen together at the right time. Saturday and Sunday would be my best days. If I was going to get him, it would be best to get him then. By the time it came round again, I'd be back in Lille. I might never see him again. If I left it until next year, I might never come back. And anyway, somebody else would have him by then. I hadn't got any time to waste. I went back to sleep, glorying in it.

Before I went out next morning, I got some new perfume and put a good dab behind each ear. I went to him every chance I got. When he was showing me something, I'd move so that his hand would brush me. I thought he was noticing me, but it wasn't until late in the afternoon that I was sure.

He was down on one knee in front of me fixing my ski. It kept coming loose. I put my knees close together and crouched a bit more. I pulled my shoulders back and filled my chest. And he noticed. He looked up, and I saw where his eyes lingered. But when they reached mine, they didn't look like how I'd thought they would. He was angry.

'Yes', he said, 'you French girls are all the same. You've got perfect bodies. You buy all the best perfumes. And you know all the tricks how to tease a man and drive him crazy. Yes. And then what do you do?'

He stopped. He let go of my ankle and stood up.

'Fix it yourself,' he said, putting on his ski. 'You know how. I've told you enough times. I've got to go down below.'

He gave himself a mighty shove-off and shot away down the slope, stabbing at the snow like a madman.

I felt like singing and shouting. He was interested, but he was afraid. He was like a little boy who'd been hurt and was afraid of being hurt again. Someone had led him on and then turned him down. It was lovely. It told me he hadn't got anybody. All I had to do was to show him I wasn't teasing him. I'd give him all the love he wanted for the rest of his life. I wouldn't care how many children we had. They'd all be lovely ones.

He avoided me for the rest of the day. I didn't chase him. I thought I'd give him time.

I went down after dinner. I thought he might come in, and he did. We had two dances, and he said he was sorry. Things had been getting in his hair a bit. He was a good dancer, but I didn't stay very long. I thought it better not to. I wanted him to think I was offended.

He was nervous and tense on Friday. When I asked him something, he'd say he was too busy. I'd have to come back later. So I did. I caught him alone late in the afternoon. We were up on the top. I checked to see that there was no one near. They had all gone down. I told him I was still having trouble with my balance: I thought it was my hips.

He was behind me with a hand on each side, pressing me forward and down.

'It's the same old thing,' he said. 'You're holding them too stiff.'

I relaxed and let myself go back into him. I heard his little gasp. His hands tightened. I leaned my head back so it nestled into his shoulder. I snuggled it in. I knew he'd get my perfume. I was getting it myself.

'Oh, Hans,' I murmured. 'You're so strong. Your hands are so warm. I love the feel of them on me.'

They slid round onto my stomach and up to my waist. He gripped tight and pulled me back into him.

'Stop it, Anna,' he whispered. 'You're driving me crazy. What are you trying to do?'

I pressed back harder and arched my back. I moved my elbows out a little from my sides. And suddenly it was just like in my dream. I knew he was going to. And he did. His hands came up and claimed me. He was gentle, but oh so possessive. It thrilled me. It told me he'd wanted to. I knew he wouldn't be satisfied. He'd want more. He'd be mine. I

ANNE ANGELO

wanted to turn to him then. But I didn't. I had to wait. Mother had told me I'd have to fight against my love when I found it. I'd have to fight against it and wait until I was married. If I didn't, I'd lose it. It wouldn't last. I'd only make misery for myself and my baby.

I brought my hands up and put them on his and pressed his to me. I loved what he was doing, and I wanted him to know it and he was welcome.

'Oh, Hans,' I said. 'That's lovely. It sends thrills right through me. I wanted you to do it, but I didn't know it would be like this. Oh, but gently, darling. It's marvellous.'

'Oh, Anna cherie. You're perfect. You're so firm and proud. You're just driving me crazy. We can't go on like this. I can't sleep for thinking about you. Anna, let's get married. Let's go to Geneva and get married. We can get away tomorrow night. There's a man there can do it for us. I'm off on Sunday. We can have the day there and come back in the evening. Will you? Oh, Anna, I swear you'll never be sorry. I'll make you happy. We'll have a proper honeymoon when the season is over. Will you? Oh, Anna, say you will?'

Of course I said I would. My heart was singing the greatest song it had ever sung. We arranged that I'd wait for him in the lounge after dinner. We'd get back in time for dinner on the Sunday. We'd keep it a secret.

That evening was the craziest I've ever had. It was turmoil. I didn't know anything. Mother had said I would. But I didn't. Should I take a nightie? Would I need one? Would he have anything? Would he think I was silly if I did? How would we get undressed? If it was one room, would we keep our backs turned? We'd have to have the light on. We could hardly drop our things anywhere. If he was in bed first, would he watch me? Of course he would. And there'd have to be a time when. Well, I couldn't put a nightie on until I'd taken the other things off, could I? I'd have my back to him. But suppose he said, 'Don't put that nightie on. Come here just as you are.' I couldn't do it. Not with the light on. I burned with hot blushes thinking about it. And I would have to go across and put the light out. He'd be watching me. And then I thought, what if the bathroom's down the hall? That decided me. I'd take a nightie, a few toilet things, and my perfume.

Before I went out on that marvellous morning, I asked Bonne-maman if I could have the Sunday off. I told her I wanted to go to Geneva. There was a trip organised to see some special ski films. There'd be champions there to explain them to us. And there'd be practical demonstrations on the Sunday. We'd all be staying over and getting back in time for Sunday dinner. Hans thought I ought to go. It would be good for me.

'Hans, my dear?' she said. 'And who is Hans?'

'Hans Bjorgsen, my instructor. He's organised it.'

'Well now, isn't that nice?'

'I think there's a child-minding service here at the hotel,' I said. 'I'll try and get someone to look after Gilbertee for the day. I don't mind paying for it. Will it be all right with you? I'd very much like to go if I could.'

'And so you shall, my dear. And so you shall. You deserve a day off. You've been very good. By all means, go and enjoy yourself. And you don't have to worry about Gilbertee. I'll look after him myself. We're not going to Evian again until Monday. I need a rest. When do you expect to get away?'

'After dinner tonight. We're all meeting in the lounge. Thank you, Bonne-maman. You're always so good to me.'

I vowed whatever happened, I wasn't going to let her down. I'd stay on until she got somebody else. I'd even stay until I got big if I had to. Hans wouldn't mind. He could carry on.

I stayed away from him all that day. The one time we did get near, our hands touched in a quick squeeze that said everything. The look in his eyes thrilled me.

I was in my room after dinner. I was putting on the final touches. My little bag was all packed and ready down by my feet. Bonne-maman was in her room going through the magazines. The dividing door was open. I'd just reached for my perfume and taken the top off.

'Are you still there, Anne?'

'Yes, Bonne-maman.'

'Are you taking anything with you, my dear?'

'Yes, Bonne-maman. I'm taking a nightie and a few toilet things. I thought I should.'

'Yes, my dear, and I think you should too. You can never tell. By the way, I met Mrs Bjorgsen, your instructor's wife, this morning. She's nice, my dear. You'd like her. They've got three children. The boy's a year younger than our Gilbertee. I went to see if there was room for another one to Geneva. I thought I'd like to go. But she didn't know anything about it. She said someone had got things mixed up. There was nothing going to Geneva tonight except her husband. He was going on business, and he was going alone. She said she'd know. She handles all the tours and bookings. Do you think you'd better go down and check, my dear? Before it's too late? I'd hate to see you disappointed.'

I don't know much what happened after that. I know the top got back on my perfume. It was there next morning.

And I did go down. It was late. But I did. I went down and checked. She was Mrs Bjorgsen, all right. She was in his office doing his books. She said she always did them when he was away. I was careful what I said. I didn't want to spoil anything that wasn't already spoiled.

'No,' she said. 'There was nothing to Geneva tonight. You're the second that's asked. My husband's the only one. He had to go on business. And as far as I'm concerned, he went on his own.'

I didn't say that as far as I was concerned too, he did. But I did say that it must be a long cold drive by himself at night.

'Yes, it is,' she said. 'But he has to do it. He gets a call and simply has to go. I wish he didn't. It always tires him out. But he's told me about you. You're one of his best pupils. He says you're coming along very nicely. And how about you? Are you satisfied with the instruction? Do you feel you're learning anything?'

'Oh yes, Mrs Bjorgsen,' I said. 'Oh yes, indeed. He's taught me such a lot. There's nobody could have taught me as much as he has. I'm more than satisfied.'

The phone rang just then, so I left.

The next morning, I told Bonne-maman I wasn't going skiing. I hadn't slept well and had a headache.

'Nonsense, my dear,' she said. 'Of course you will. It's the best thing for you. The fresh air will do you good. Oh, but you can't, can you? You'll have no instructor. He mightn't be back for days.' She thought for a moment. 'That's no good. We'll have to see if we can get you someone else. Come along. Let's get to them before they're all booked out. This might be a very good thing, my dear. A different instructor will have a different approach. You'll get a wider experience.'

And he did have a different approach, different altogether. He was like a lovely old uncle. It didn't take him very long before he said there was nothing wrong with either my style or my hips. He wished he was twenty years younger. He said I had the nicest pair of hips he'd seen around the place for many a long day.

'You've got nothing to worry about, mam'selle. You're doing very well. If you've only been skiing for the few days you say, you've got the makings of a champion. There's no doubt about young Bjorgsen. He can certainly handle beginners. Especially girls and young women. He's taught you a lot. There's one thing, though. It seems to me you're favouring your left foot. That's not good. Your weight has got to be even. Let's take a run down. You go ahead so I can watch.'

Gilbertee and I both changed over to him. Bonne-maman arranged it. She said there was no trouble. Mr Bjorgsen was most understanding and gave her a refund. He and I passed each other lots of times, but we never spoke.

We took a different route coming home. Bonne-maman had friends at Morez in France in the mountains just over the border from Switzerland. We took the road along the north shore of Lac Leman to Nyon. There we turned right and took the shortcut up into the mountains. It was crazy with sharp hairpin bends and zigzags. Gustave had all he could do to get the big Packard up and round some of them. At St Cerque on the summit, we crossed the frontier into France to les Rousses and Morez. We had lunch there. We got back onto the road to Dijon through Champagnole and Dole.

We stayed overnight at Dijon. This was where they had the gorgeous big chateau. They had stables too, thoroughbred stables. We stayed so I could go riding. I'd never ridden a thoroughbred before. I'd only had pony rides in Invergordon. This was nothing like that. He was a perfect thing, sleek and shining with grooming, so gentle and docile yet surging with power. The saddle and bridle shone from years of care and attention. I realised what my mother's life must have been like before she met Father. Mont-de-Marsan and Perigueux must have been like this.

At Cambrai, I picked up my two parasols, and we were home a week before the children got back from their schools.

The feeling I'd had up on the top there at Lausanne never left me. I'd looked down on them all and realised I'd arrived. I was as good as any of them. And I was too. I was better in some ways. The only real difference was that they had money, lots of money. I knew I could get money if I wanted to. But I didn't want to. Bonne-maman was like a mother to me. I was perfectly happy. I had everything I wanted. I didn't really want to get mixed up with men. They were too dangerous, and I carried too much of a traitor in my own heart. With Toshack and Geordie McPhail and Father, I'd had to fight. I'd seen the danger. With Hans, I hadn't seen any danger. In fact, I'd gone after him. I understood what had happened to my mother better. But for Bonne-maman, I'd have been in a worse mess. I'd have been on my way to joining Les Misérables loitering in furtive doorways to get money any way I could for myself. I couldn't expect her to be on hand next time to save me.

*   *   *

CHAPTER 16

St Malo

I HAD NO NEED to worry. My near-disaster at Lausanne had convinced Bonne-maman I was an utter babe in the woods. She had no intention of leaving my future in my own hands nor for Nature to arrange things. She would attend to it herself before I made a complete hash of everything. She took me for what amounted to a crash course in mothercraft and childcare. Then, when she thought I'd absorbed the rudiments, she brought the most eligible male she could find to view me in the most attractive setting—playing mother to hordes of children. He was a nephew or something once removed. She was careful to tell me he was the only son of a very wealthy branch of the family. It was a pity there were other things about him she didn't know.

But there were things about me she didn't know either. So I suppose we broke even on that. She didn't know, for instance, that it had been me who'd set out to catch Hans. She thought it was the other way around. And she didn't know about Toshack and Geordie McPhail. Nor about Father and his treatment of Mother and his plans for me. You don't tell things like that to people you want to respect you. Especially not people like Bonne-maman. So she naturally saw me as a brand to be plucked from the burning.

It was at Easter in the following spring, 1935. We went for the ten days to the Cote d'Emeraude. It was a kind of holiday camp for all her grandchildren. There were swarms and regiments of them.

The Cote d'Emeraude, the Emerald Coast, is part of the Gulf of St Malo on the central west coast. The Gulf is pointed in the north by the Cap de la Hague and in the west by Perros-Guirez. Between these two arms, it embraces the British Islands of Jersey, Guernesey, and

Sark. It faces across the English Channel to Dartmouth, Plymouth, and Land's End. The Cote d'Emeraude is that select portion centred between Granville and Paimpol.

Bonne-maman had three villas at St Lunaire. St Lunaire sprawls on a headland between St Malo and St Cast in the cream of the cream of that select central portion. Her three villas clung to the rocks overlooking the sea.

Each Easter, her children and their spouses brought their offspring and their governesses to her and went off for holidays on their own. Their houses were shut up so their staffs could go for their holidays at the same time. It was Bonne-maman's way of giving the parents a break and getting all her grandchildren together for some character building. She made them mix. She taught them to be useful. A family is a small society. It has to be organised. Everyone has to make some effort for the common good. Woe to anyone who shirked or deliberately broke the rules, remembering of course, that children are only children.

We went ahead to prepare. There was much to be done before the invasion. The Packard was crammed and piled with bags and bundles of all shapes and sizes. Jammed in amongst them Bonne-maman, her cook, the four children, and I were barely visible.

We got to Amiens for lunch and Rouen for the night. Inevitably, she had relatives there. From Rouen we pressed on to reach Caen for an early lunch. Bonne-maman had a problem. It involved distance, time, and desire. It was to be in time for lunch at Caen and yet be able to get to St Malo in good time for afternoon tea.

Two elderly English spinsters ran a teashop there. The atmosphere was that of a garden tea party at Buckingham Palace. They spoke with the purest of pure Oxford accents and had absolutely impeccable manners. They served oven-fresh wholemeal bread and dairy butter, cottage cream cheese and shrimps, and strawberry jam and cider. For Bonne-maman, a whiff of Buckingham Palace was not a thing to be lightly missed.

So with an imperious dowager accustomed to having her every wish, separated from her heart's desire by a long drive from the only suitable lunching place, hindered in her progress by children requiring stops at every sizeable clump of bushes along the way, there was a problem.

For poor Gustave, it was a nightmare. A steady driver, he was forced to speed because of the time factor and the long distance between lunch and target. An added strain to this recklessness was the need to keep a watch for sizeable clumps. Inevitably, he overshot and had to back up. This took time. Which he had to go even faster to make up for. Which meant he overshot farther at the next clump. With a longer backup. Tick, tick, tick, the time flew. 'Nightmare' was the only word.

Fortunately, it was only a short drive after afternoon tea from St Malo back along and over the water to get to St Lunaire. By then, of course, Bonne-maman was in a wonderfully serene and contented mood.

Everything had been organised in advance. There were rosters for every detail involving each child expected to roll up. Everyone over four had to do something—bed making, room cleaning, washing and ironing, sewing and mending, darning socks, doing potatoes, helping cook, weeding flowerbeds, helping Gustave-cum-gardener. Bigger ones bossed smaller ones, and bigger ones bossed them. The chain of responsibility went up through me to her. Her organising was so reliable there wasn't a hitch. The upcoming sun set the hive humming. A fixed period was set aside each morning for 'devoirs de vacances'—homework preparation for next term's school.

Lunch was at twelve sharp. At one o'clock, everybody had to be on their bed with a rug over them. It was surprising to me, going round checking, how quickly sleep prevailed.

At 2 p.m., a bell in each villa brought them all to the tables reaching at plates of freshly baked wholemeal buns sliced and filled with cottage cream cheese. There was as much milk, fresh from the cows that morning, as they could drink. Then their governesses were in charge, and it was helter-skelter. Children going in all directions. To this pool where the little crabs lived. To that pool where the small fishes were. To the bigger pools to paddle and fall down to get gloriously wet and dirty. Around to the rocks to find things no one had ever seen before. And to carefully carry them home to keep to show Bonne-maman and me. There'd be bumps and abrasions to be kissed and made better. And things to be got out of eyes. Therese was left in charge of our crowd.

By two fifteen, Bonne-maman, Gustave, and I would be away. We'd go up and down the coast seeking the best buys in fish, lobsters, shellfish, and whatever else caught her fancy. Always keeping in mind, of course, the need to be within reach of her Buckingham Palace at the proper time.

Afterwards, serene and beneficent, she'd take me through the narrow winding streets to find the little shops run by sweet old ladies selling the fine Breton lace. Cobbled streets so narrow no profaning motor car has ever penetrated. She showed me the massive ramparts built to keep out the invaders from the sea. Ramparts so huge and impregnable it seemed nothing could ever breach them. But where they'd been rebuilt after the seventeenth century wars and again after the eighteenth century.

Then, time no longer being a factor, we'd go far afield out into the country for the big round farm cheeses. Vegetables were dug and cut while we waited. We bought butter and eggs—chicken, duck, and goose eggs. She got the pick of the poultry, berries, flowers, and homemade cider. She made me aware of the beauty of France in the spring. It was a paradise.

In the evenings, she'd teach them to be thrifty and useful. She'd slit the worn sheets down the middle, and they'd sew the outside edges together so they'd still be usable. They did needlework, drawn-thread-work, knitted fair isle sweaters. The boys played records— quietly—and draughts and chess. It was an atmosphere of peace and contentment, far removed from the screaming and smashing of blizzards at Invergordon.

We had a visitor one afternoon towards the end of the week. It was just after the two o'clock bell. Everyone was clamouring for buns and milk. He said he was just passing through and thought he'd look in and see how we were. She introduced him as Raoule. He was from Marcq. He had the latest model MG Sports. He called it his mousetrap. He said he'd had it up to a hundred. Would I care to go for a drive?

'Of course she would,' Bonne-maman said. 'Go on, my dear. Off you go and enjoy yourself. You deserve it. You've been very good.'

But I didn't want to go with him. Why should I? He didn't look anything special. He was about thirty and smallish with a small black moustache. I doubted he'd be able to drive any better than my brother Peter, or me even. We'd had some terrific runs. And anyway, I'd be going out with her and Gustave shortly. I didn't want to miss that for the sake of a spin with him. So I told him thanks very much but maybe some other time. I had to look after the children. He buzzed off.

She said I'd been foolish. I should have gone with him.

'He's a very nice boy,' she said. 'And he came all the way from Marcq to see you. He's just what you need, my dear. He's got a good job. His family's very well off. They own mills, and he's the only child. You were very foolish. You won't do much better than Raoule.'

I knew then it'd been arranged. His story about passing through had been just that. Marcq was some 500 kilometres away, the other side of Lille. The only place he could have been passing through to that would have brought him to St Lunaire was England, across the Channel. And that would have been a very damp drive in his little mousetrap.

I didn't let on, though. I knew she meant well. She always did. She just didn't understand that I wasn't interested in men.

During our last two or three days, the various parents came and took their children home. By Monday, we only had our own family. We cleaned and tidied everything up again. M'sieu came and took his three older ones and the cook. And Bonne-maman and I went off with Gilbertee for our holiday. We took our time and wandered along the coast sightseeing. She gave me a personally conducted tour of all the best parts of Normandy and Picardy.

We went out to the Mont St Michel and then round to Avranches. Then we turned inland to Caen. Poking round in the little back shops with Bonne-maman looking for Breton lace, I found two lovely parasols. We went to Honfleur and Le Havre, where we stayed the night. And then on to Fecamp, where she had a villa. We had a week there. It was a gorgeous big place with gothic columns looking out over lovely gardens. Then we made our way home through St Valery-en-Caux, Abbeyville, and Bethune.

A few weeks later, I had a phone call from Raoule. He had a couple of seats for the opera. He'd been let down. Would I care to go? It was

Mozart's *Le Nozze di Figaro*. Of course I would. Who wouldn't? He gave me champagne with the dinner, and supper afterwards. A week or so later, it was dinner and a movie. Then it was the ballet. It was *Swan Lake* and the best seats. He was obviously interested. I gave it some thought.

He wasn't exactly my dream man. Not after Hans. He was too fussy about little things. But at least he was someone to go out with, and we did seem to have the same tastes in lots of things. It could have gone on to who knows what. But there was a rude awakening coming to me.

It was the night of the ballet. We were in his car on the drive at the back of 241 near the steps. It was perfect. The ballet had been good, and we'd had a nice supper. I was snuggled into his shoulder, revelling in the glories of the night. He had his arm round me, and the night was filled with the scent of roses and magnolia, cestrum nocturnum, and jasmine. I was utterly content. I could have stayed there until breakfast, But he gave me a squeeze and nuzzled into the back of my neck.

'Come on then,' he said. 'That's plenty. Let's go. We can't stop here all night.'

'Let's go?' I asked. 'Where to? And why can't we stay here all night?'

'Where to? Why, where do you think? Inside, of course. We don't want to waste the night sitting here in the car, do we?'

'Why on earth not? And what do you want to go inside for? There'll be nobody up. They'll all be in bed ages ago. Oh, Raoule, what's wrong with you? What else do you want? Just smell that garden and look at that perfect moon. This is just heavenly.'

'You know what I want, my little pigeon,' he breathed hotly behind my ear. 'I want you, and well you know it. Now stop playing the innocent. I haven't been mean with you, now don't you be mean with me. I've been patient. But this is a night for love. Let's go inside and enjoy it with each other.'

I freed myself and turned to face him.

'Come on,' he coaxed, trying to take my hands. 'All right, then. If you don't want to go in here, let's go to my place. I've got everything there. We can have the whole night if you like. You can stay tomorrow if you want to. I'll bring you home whenever you say. Oh, come on.'

I saw him as I'd never seen him before. I was disgusted with myself for being so blind. I got my purse and opened the door.

'No, no!' He clutched at my arm. 'Don't be like that. I know how to make love. They all say so. I'll be gentle and make you happy. Oh, come on. Be nice. She said we could do a lot for each other, and so we can. But you've got to do your share. Oh come on. Please?'

If I hadn't been so disgusted, I'd have had to laugh. He was incredible. He really thought his 'Please?' was going to do it.

I felt cleaner out on the driveway in the night air. With his door shut between us, I paused for a moment with both hands on it, looking in at him. He was pitiful. There wasn't a spark of manliness about him. I wondered how I could have been so blind. He was injured and reproachful like a little boy who's been cheated of his toffee. The mouth under the natty moustache was moist and pouting.

'I warn you, Anne', he said leaning over and looking up at me, 'if you go now, it'll be the finish. I'll never take you out again. And I mean that. You're not making a fool out of me.' He unlatched the door. 'Now come on. Get back in and don't be so silly.'

I couldn't help laughing as I turned and went inside. I was going through the foyer when I heard him start up and roar away.

But the full nastiness of him didn't strike me until later. It was gone three o'clock. I was up in my room trying to write him a letter. I wanted to send him what I thought it'd cost for my three nights out but couldn't think how to put it. I'd wasted my last sheet of notepaper, so I scrapped the idea. Let him say what he liked. He would, anyway.

And then it struck me that as likely as not, he'd say I hadn't cheated him. That really burned me up. I'd met a lot of his friends. They'd talk, and he'd have to brag. They'd likely pass their cast-offs along to each other. I wondered what happened to the poor creatures when they were finished with them.

And I wondered if that was the usual thing: three nights out and then expect payment. It made me so disgusted with men that I decided they weren't worth the bother. If I wanted to go out in future, I'd pay my own way.

Bonne-maman noticed I wasn't going out and asked me what was

ANNE ANGELO

wrong. I didn't want to tell her. After all, he was her relative. But she insisted. So I just told her what I had to. She guessed the rest.

'Oh, my dear,' she said. 'I am sorry. So that's why he's never married, is it? I never dreamed he was like that. I'm afraid I've done you more harm than good. I promise you I'll never interfere again.'

*　　*　　*

CHAPTER 17

Monte Carlo

I KNEW SHE'D MEANT well. Of course I did. She meant well in everything she did. But that didn't alter the effect. It burned in. For months I didn't go out anywhere. Except round to her place and maybe for a few quick shopping trips. I didn't want to go out. I felt that everywhere I went, I was being talked about. I imagined them pointing me out and sniggering. It was horrible. So I just didn't go out.

I spent a lot of time at her place. She taught me about investing.

She'd found out I was putting money in the bank.

'That's foolish, my dear,' she said. 'It'll do you no good there. The interest they pay doesn't even keep up with the inflation rate. You lose money every day it's there. You should invest it. I'll show you if you like. You'll be surprised how it'll grow.'

She did show me, and I was surprised. I did so well I became interested. I realised I could be independent. I didn't really need any man.

If things had happened the other way round, if I'd met Raoule before I met Hans, my life could have been very different. I could've forgotten the nastiness and been left with my memories of Hans. Although he was married, he was perfect. The answer to any girl's dream. I'd have been looking for someone like him.

At Monte Carlo, I got the sort of chance that only comes once in a lifetime. I met a fine man who wanted to marry me. He was a millionaire, and he was sincere. If I'd married him, I'd never have wanted for anything for the rest of my life. But I didn't. I wasn't interested. It wouldn't have mattered if he'd been Adonis himself. It would have been simply marrying him for his money. And I was doing so well I didn't feel I had to do that.

It was in the late summer of that same year, 1935. The three of us—Bonne-maman, Gilbertee, and I—went to Monaco with Gustave in the Packard. The children had been home and gone back to their schools again. We had a fortnight there.

We went down through the centre and stayed at the places we'd been to on our way to Switzerland. Except that it was a very different France. It was a France sweltering in the full heat, sweltering and burgeoning with the labour of harvest.

I'd never seen such heat. As the girls had said, in my warm Scottish clothes, I 'would have cooked, yes?' Cars approaching us on the roads seemed to float free from the ground until they were quite close up. The earth and the road shimmered in the heat. The eyes were sore peering against it. The air was drowsy with the hum of millions of bees. Gustave had to drive slower to avoid killing so many of them on the windscreen. Herds of black and white Friesians sought shelter from the blazing sun whenever they could find it. Somewhere along the road, we stopped by the grape pickers, and they filled our basket with great bunches of luscious fruit. There were the big iron gates with the huge gold-painted 'H' on them. And the long driveway meandering away over the rise to where the chateau stood, half concealed among the trees. I don't know whether it was the home of Heidsieck—the world's most famous champagne makers, or whether it was for Hennessy, the equally renowned Cognac distillers.

In Lyon, instead of turning towards Chamberry and Geneva, we kept straight on for Valence for our third night.

As we got farther south, the heat was almost overpowering. It was more, even, than Nature herself could stand. Great black thunderheads piled up until the burden became too great. Then she exploded them in awesome fury. Lightning and thunder split and crashed at the same moment. We scurried into Avignon in a torrential downpour.

Bonne-maman didn't like travelling in the rain. So we stopped for lunch and hoped it would pass. But it didn't. It settled into a steamy drizzle that lasted for three days. So we stayed there in Avignon. It must have been her favourite city because she knew every nook and cranny of it. I discovered how deeply religious she was. She knew the details of every one of the beautiful gothic churches and cathedrals. She told me all their histories. She showed me the defences round the city. Defences built by the five popes who had lived there and protected the city through the ages. In spite of the steamy weather, there wasn't a dull moment.

From Avignon, we pressed on through Aix-en-Provence to get to Brignoles by midday. From there we were within easy reach of the coast and St Raphael, Cannes, Nice, and Monaco.

No other name but Cote d'Azure—the Blue Coast—would fit it. It was the most gorgeously beautiful blue. Villas of every imaginable shade dotted along the hillsides made it an artist's paradise. The yachts on the water looked like toys. Some were ridiculously tiny, while others were coarse in their gross ostentation.

That first time at the Monte Carlo Casino proved again to me what I'd learned at the Winter Sports in Lausanne. I had no need to feel inferior to anybody. I was better than lots of the people I met there. And monied people too. I watched them get carried away and make fools of themselves. I didn't do that. And it was all because of her and her coaching.

We were in her flat in Monaco. She had a lovely flat at No. 3 Suffren Raymonde, getting ready to go. I wasn't keen. Mother'd always taught us gambling was bad: it undermined character. Bonne-maman said that was rubbish. I'd gambled when I came to France. They'd gambled when they'd had me. Most of life's a gamble.

'All your investments are gambles,' she said. 'The thing is to know when to gamble. See what the odds are against you and see if the possible returns justify the risk. You don't go tonight expecting to win. That way lies disaster. You go for a night out to enjoy yourself. You only take what you can afford to lose. Sometimes you get cleaned out quickly. Sometimes you have a marvellous lot of fun. Sometimes you even come home with some of their money. But you'll see what gambling does to people. And people you'd have thought intelligent too. If you're lucky, you'll lose. If not, you'll win. But we'll see. I hope you lose.'

I couldn't figure that out—lucky and lose, unlucky and win? But she explained.

She'd taken one of her nephews to the casino some years before, and he'd won. He'd won enough to go back home and put a down payment on a house and get married. He'd thought he was lucky, but she said it had ruined him. He was only twenty-four. He was the accountant with one of the family companies. That first win gave him an appetite. Gambling got into his blood. He altered the books and dibbed into the company funds. In the end, he was disgraced and became an outcast. She didn't even know where he'd got to.

'It's not unusual,' she said. 'It's happening all the time. People who start off by winning, naturally think they can do it again. The more times they win, the bigger the hold it gets over them. They have to lose in the end. Everyone has to. Only the casino can win. It can't go wrong.'

I asked her, did she mean it wasn't honest, that it was all rigged.

'Oh no, I don't say that,' she said. 'All the machines are checked. And the dealers deal properly. It's the odds that are not right. Let us put it this way. Suppose a hundred people go in with a thousand francs each. At the end of a night's play, some will have won, and some will have lost. But if you got all those people together and checked how much they had, you would find they hadn't got the hundred thousand they went in with. The casino would have a large share of it. And if they went back and played for a few more nights, they wouldn't have any of it. The casino would have the lot. It has to.

'The building has to be paid for and maintained. The croupiers and the dealers, the security guards and the money changers have to be paid. They have to be provided with expensive uniforms. All the luxurious furnishings and carpets and the paintings on the walls all cost money. The company has to pay dividends to its shareholders. It all has to come out of the pockets of the people who go there and play.

'It's the same with horseracing or any other form of organised gambling. With racing, the horses have to be bought and fed and trained. The trainers and jockeys and the bookmakers and the touts, the gardeners and the cleaners all have to get a living. The racing club has to get its share. And it has to pay taxes to the Government.

'It's done by altering the odds. Say there were fifty horses in a race. And fifty people put one franc on one horse to win—each one bet on a different horse. The winning horse should pay fifty to one. But it wouldn't. You'd be lucky if it paid twenty-five to one. The rest would have gone to pay for all the things I've mentioned.

'At the roulette, you'll see that all the bets on the table don't go to the winning number. Nothing like it. The croupier rakes in a big share. That's why I say gamblers can't win. It's not possible.'

Having her put it like that made a big difference when we got there. I wasn't over-awed, as I saw lots of people were. The magnificent doorman in his splendid clothes was only a paid servant. People like me paid him his wages and bought that uniform. It was the same when we got inside. As she'd said, it was a marvellous place. Money was no object. But it was money that came from people like me.

I learned from the people I saw too. Some of them were unmistakably wealthy—rings and jewellery and expensive furs—but they didn't have much sense. They had notebooks and made notes of where the ball went for every play. Bonne-maman told me afterwards that they were there every night. They tried to work out systems how to beat the game. As if where the ball went last time made any difference to where it would go next time. The wheel spins one way, and the ball goes the opposite way. No one can tell where it will stop.

'I only bet small. I had a few wins, but in the end, they got it all back. Then I went for a look around by myself. I learned a lot about people. For all their wealth, some of them were such poor creatures.

'It was on our third night I met Wilmer J. Hoxton. He was American. He'd been watching me, but I didn't know. He was on the other side of Bonne-maman. I'd just placed my last bet and lost. I was going to go for my wander around, but Bonne-maman touched my arm.

'"No, dear. Don't go," she said. "Here." She put some counters down in front of me. "Mr Hoxton said would you play these for him. He thinks your luck's due to change. It won't matter if you lose."

I looked at him, and he looked all right. He was about fifty. He was clean looking and nice. He smiled and nodded. She seemed to think it was all right. So I did. And I won and kept on winning. It was terrific. I was still winning when we stopped. They were all watching me. I pushed it all to him and thanked him. It'd been great fun. But he wanted me to take some for myself. I said no. It wasn't mine. I'd only played for him.

We all went for supper together. He was nice. He was from Texas. He had a cattle ranch, and they were drilling for oil. He was on his own. He'd lost his wife and family in a motor smash nearly twenty years ago. He said he came to Monte Carlo a lot. He and Bonne-maman got on well together. It was lovely. He took us everywhere. He had a yacht and a Rolls-Royce. He was often at the flat. It wasn't until the day before we were due to leave that I found out the truth.

We'd arranged to go up into the Alps Maritime. He wanted to show us the flower-growing areas around Grasse and St Valiers. We were going to take a basket and go for the day. But on the morning, Bonne-maman had a headache, so only the two of us went.

We went up along the coast past Nice and turned inland. It was marvellous. You could smell the perfume long before we saw anything. There were miles and miles of roses and mimosa. He told me it takes one million rose petals to make one ounce of attar-of-roses. Attar-of-roses is the basis of most perfumes.

He'd brought a lovely lunch, champagne on ice and everything. And he asked me to marry him. He said he'd asked Bonne-maman, and she had no objections. He thought she was my guardian. I didn't say she wasn't. I told him I'd have to ask her. And that's how we left it.

She thought I should accept.

'It would be a very good thing for you, my dear,' she said. 'I don't want to lose you. I've grown very fond of you. But I don't want to stand in your way either. It's a chance you won't get again. He's sincere, and he must be a millionaire several times over. You'll never ever want for anything. He said he doesn't mind if you have children. He's fifty-six, and by the time he's gone, your children would be growing up round you. And you could soon find somebody else. You'd be a very wealthy widow. You think about it very carefully.'

And I did. I was awake a long time thinking about it. But it wasn't what I wanted. I didn't want to get married or anything. I was happy enough as I was. Texas was a long way away. I didn't know anything about it. I might get out there, and something might go wrong. And I'd be on my own. Here, with Bonne-maman and the family, I knew I'd always be looked after. I liked France, and I didn't want for anything. Why should I marry him just because he was a millionaire? He was nice, but I didn't have any feelings for him. Not like I'd had with Hans. It didn't seem fair to him either. I'd only be marrying him for his money. So in the morning I told him no and we came back to Lille.

*　　*　　*

CHAPTER 18

The Depression Hits

BUT THE TIME came when I wished I hadn't been quite so offhand with Wilner J. If I'd had his address, I'd have written to him, although by that time, it would probably have been too late. Things happened which I hadn't foreseen. Everybody knew Germany was on the move, but I hadn't dreamt it could affect me. I'd been accepted into a large and wealthy family. It was well established. So long as I served the family properly, nothing could go wrong. It's possible Bonne-maman had tried to give me the hint when she'd advised me about Wilmer. I don't know. But when it came, it came as a rude awakening.

Everything went smoothly until Easter 1937. She and I went everywhere and had our usual holidays. My parasol collection grew. The children came home and went back. Therese got married and went off. Nicole was engaged. Gilbertee was no longer the cherub with the golden curls.

We were in St Lunaire for the yearly get-together with the grandchildren. It was the last day, and M'sieu came to pick up his three. And my world suddenly crumbled and fell to pieces. The depression had caught up with him.

He said he'd had to make changes. He wouldn't be at 241 anymore. Things were too uncertain. He'd shifted to Paris. He'd bought a house. It was smaller, and there was only room for the cook and one maid. He'd have to let the rest of us go. He'd pay me three months in advance, and it would give me time to look for something else. If I wanted to, I could stay on at 241 until the time was up. He was going to sell or let it. If he couldn't, in that time, he'd close it up. And he gave me the

Buick. He said I'd looked after it so well I deserved it. Then he took his children and left us.

Its utter unexpectedness gave us a shock. Bonne-maman and I didn't go for our usual lovely wander up along the coast. We came straight home. Home? It was no longer my home. It was a house I was living in on borrowed time.

They were all gone. Except Marie-Louise who was left in charge with one maid to help her. He'd taken all his personal things but left the furniture and furnishings. Marie-Louise had brought in her old uncle Jacques to do the gardening, and her nephew young Jacques for the odd jobs. He was a radical who'd dropped out from the university.

It was impossible to get another place. I tried everywhere. I supposed it was because I was older. They preferred younger ones. And everyone was getting nervous about Germany. Lots of the wealthier families were getting out of the north of France. I wrote everywhere to people I'd met but no one knew of anything. Bonne-maman tried all her friends, but it was no good. I put an advertisement in the local papers.

> Governess seeks engagement. Refined Scottish lady,
> 23, with English, French and Latin, last position 3 years,
> will go anywhere, very fond of children.

Days drifted, time melted away. I sent my ad to Paris. Then all over France from Lille to Marseille and from Nantes in the west to Belfort in the east. In desperation, I sent it across to the *London Times*.

A month went with no response. We were halfway through the second time before anything stirred. It came from Monte Carlo and on casino-beaded paper. It said if I could call for an interview, something might be arranged.

'If I could call for an interview?' The Buick got me there in three days. But he wasn't there. He was on holiday and wouldn't be back until the Monday week. That was on the Friday. They said to be there at eleven o'clock.

It was too far to go back to Lille, so I stayed at Bonne-maman's flat.

ANNE ANGELO

I had a lovely ten days lazing around the beaches. I hoped I might see Wilder or somebody. But I didn't. There were only the wolves.

I was at the casino at eleven sharp on the Monday. Mr Gugliemo was already in his office. He was pleased when he knew what I'd come about. He had my ad in his drawer. He pulled it out and studied it and me. He was Italian, short and stocky, about forty, and well dressed. He said it wasn't for himself. It was for his brother who lived in Ventimiglia, just over the border in Italy.

'You like to live in Italy?' he asked, watching me.

I told him I didn't care where I lived. His English wasn't very good, but I didn't let on I knew any Italian. I thought it was better for him to struggle in English than for me to struggle in Italian. And in thinking like that, although I didn't know it at the time, I saved myself from the worst blunder I could ever have made in my entire life.

In my desperation, I put my cards on the table. I didn't expect any more replies. I had to get this job if I possibly could. I told him I had to get out of where I was. I had to find somewhere to live. I had no folks to go to. I was willing to go anywhere. It didn't matter where it was. That pleased him too.

He asked me if I liked fruit. I told him I did. He said that was good. His brother had lots of fruit. He had the big orchard.

But he had trouble with my word 'engagement'. 'Governess seeks engagement.' He wanted to know what I meant. We spent a lot of time on that. I tried to explain it meant a job, a position, work, but he wasn't happy about it. We were getting nowhere. So I said maybe it might be better if I could meet his brother. We could see if we suited each other. I didn't want to risk missing out on the job on account of a misunderstanding. He said his brother was at Ventimiglia. It was twenty-five kilometres away. I said that was nothing. I had the Buick outside. If he'd give me the address, I could be there in an hour.

'You gotta the motor car?' he said. He was surprised.

I told him I had. He wanted to see it. So I took him out and showed him. He walked all round it, examining the paintwork. He looked inside. He kicked the tyres. Then he asked if it was really mine. I told him it was. And that finished it. He patted me on the shoulder and said

I'd do very well. He was sure his brother would be pleased. He'd take me to him straight away. He'd just go in and get his coat and tell them he was going. He wouldn't be a minute.

The clock on the casino said 11.42. I felt so happy I took its photo. I thought my troubles were over. I'd have it as a souvenir.

He came bustling out, struggling into his coat, and away we went.

He said I could call him Giuseppe. His brother's name was Pepito. 'I call him Peppi,' he said. 'You will like him. Everybody like Peppi. He'sa the big man in Ventimiglia. You will be happy with him. He'sa bigger than me and very strong. He's older too. He'sa forty-five. You notta worry.' He patted my knee. 'It will be all right.'

I saw the border control post in the distance and remembered I didn't have my passport with me. I hadn't expected to be leaving France. But he said not to worry.

'I fix it,' he said, again patting my knee. 'These'a Doganieri—they know me. They come to the casino. I do things for them. They make no trouble. I fix it. You stay here.'

He went in as if he owned the place. There was great laughing and going on. Some of them came to the door and had a look at me, but no one said anything. They were all still laughing when he came out. When we'd got away, I asked him what he'd said, but he only laughed and said it was nothing.

We were still out in the country when he told me to turn in between sagging gateposts. A narrow dirt track wound in through tall grass. A broken gate leaned round to one side. We bumped and bounced over potholes and tree roots. I slowed down to a crawl. There were stumps and fallen trees half buried in the growths. Other dead trees still stood, their jagged arms held starkly to the heavens. The sun hid its face, and suddenly the day was colder.

We came to some buildings standing back around a clearing. There was a big packing shed and some smaller sheds. An old weather-beaten house had one end of its verandahs collapsed and resting on the ground. There was a wisp of smoke from its chimney. Everything looked run-down and neglected. Doors sagged from one hinge. Windows were empty black eye sockets. Stacks of dirty old fruit cases leaned against each other and against the sheds. There was an old cart with one wheel off, with its rear axle propped up on fruit cases. The wheel was on the ground with grass growing up between its spokes. Tins and bottles lay everywhere, rusty four-gallon tins squashed and battered into all sorts of shapes, food and jam tins with bits of the labels still stuck on.

There were children. I counted twelve. They were the grubbiest, scruffiest, uncared-for lot I'd ever seen. The biggest was a girl about fourteen: the smallest a toddler no more than a baby. Not one of them had seen soap and water in weeks. Their hair hadn't been brushed nor combed. Their clothes were in rags and filthy. They were all barefoot. The toddler was as naked as the day he was born. Flies were feeding round their eyes and on the food or whatever it was round their mouths. They made me shudder.

They came so close I had to stop. He got out and spoke to them. I didn't hear what was said, but the biggest girl went off reluctantly and into the house. He came round to my side.

'Come on,' he said. 'You can leave it. It will be all right.'

I didn't like it one little bit. It looked so awful. But I switched off, got my purse, and got out. They stared at me as if I'd come from another world. Grubby little hands reached out to finger my dress. The toddler plonked himself down and sat tracing round my high heels with a dirty little forefinger.

I asked Mr Gugliemo whose they were and where their mother was.

He said they were his brother's. The mothers were all gone.

'Peppi have bad luck,' he said. 'Six months now he have to do it all himself. First he have Rosa. But she no good. She come from Ventimiglia. Rosa lazy. She only have three and then she say too much work, too many babies, she going home to her mamma. And she go.'

'Then he get Carlotta. Carlotta good but too old. She come from Roma. She have three and then can't have any more. Peppi have to send her back to Roma.

'Then Maria, she come. Maria was the best. She come from Cassino. Maria was strong. She can do everything. She have seven. But then she hurt herself fixing the cart.' He gestured to where the wheel lay on the ground. 'Just after she have the baby. He send her to hospital, but it no good. She die. But now it will be all right. You soon fix everything. You are young and strong. You soon make it nice. Come on. We go to the house.'

He started off across, but I didn't see any sense in it. Yes, I might be young and strong, but this wasn't my sort of place. I was a governess, not a charwoman. It was all so squalid and hopeless. It would need an army to fix it. I looked round at it again. I looked at the children. I felt like getting in and driving away.

He stopped, looking back and waiting.

'Come on,' he called. 'You want to see Peppi? He'sa in the house. You come and see him. He'sa fixing the baby.'

I thought, *All right. I've come so far, I'll go and see him. But it'll be a waste of time. I could never live in a place like this.*

When he saw I was coming, he went off again. But I hadn't gone far before my heel went through a tin. I had to balance on one foot to get the tin off without damaging the heel. I was just putting the shoe on again when I saw his brother come out to the door. He had to be his brother, and he was grotesque.

He hadn't shaved for days. He was barefoot and dirtier than the children. He only had a ragged shirt and pants on, and they looked as if he'd lived in them for months. The shirt was stained and didn't have a button on it. It hung open, showing a bulging fat stomach. The sleeves were gone at the elbows. The trousers were tied with string and had been torn off just below the knees. He had a low forehead like an ape. He was covered with black hair. He looked like a horrible hairy baboon.

'What's the matter with you, Giuseppe?' he shouted angrily in Italian. 'Don't you think I've got any work to do? What do you want this time?'

His brother stopped dead with his feet braced, his fists on his hips, and his head up.

'Calla miseria porca, Peppi!' he shouted back. It too was in Italian. 'What's wrong with you? You want the woman, don't you? Well, I've got a woman for you. Mio Dio! I've got a woman like you've never had before. She's young, and she's good-looking. She's got the good figure. She's rich. She's got the motor car. And she can't go home. She's got no home to go to. She comes from France. Madonna Mia! You'll be all right this time. You take her now, eh? I'll go to town and get some wine. We'll make it your birthday.'

As I turned and ran, I thanked heaven for that tin. It'd given me a start on them. And I thanked heaven for my bit of Italian. Without it, I'd have walked right in there unsuspecting. Life would have become a never-ending nightmare.

I managed to get the car started and turned before they reached me. I couldn't drive fast and get away: there were too many bottles.

He got up on the running board, trying to get the door open.

'What's the matter with you, you crazy woman?' he panted, tugging and wrenching. I held it tight and drove with one hand. 'We not going to hurt you. Peppi, he give you all you want. He give you everything. What's the matter with you?'

I told him he was wrong. That wasn't what I wanted at all. It was all a misunderstanding. I just wanted to go back to France.

That made him really angry.

'You've only been making the fools of us, eh? Well, you're not so smart. You won't get away. I told them you're his wife. You'd run away and I was bringing you back. They won't let you through. We'll get you. Better you stop now and not be so silly.'

I tried to brush him off against a dead tree, but he saw it coming and jumped clear. He ran behind me shouting rude things in Italian.

I was going into Ventimiglia before I realised what I'd done. I'd turned the wrong way. Instead of getting out of Italy I was going farther in. I pulled over and stopped. I found I was trembling.

I was in a trap.

If I went back they might be there waiting for me. I wouldn't be able to just run them over. And if I did get through, I wouldn't get past the border. If I tried to cross the border somewhere else, I wouldn't be able to without a passport. They'd probably hold me as an illegal immigrant. They'd hold me and deport me, probably back to Scotland. I'd be back in Father's hands. And if I went ahead, they might be waiting for me. They might have rung through. I didn't know if they had the telephone.

I hadn't seen any wires, but that didn't mean a thing. There wouldn't be many Buicks like mine.

And I couldn't stop where I was. They might stop someone and come after me. I kept an eye on the mirror.

I decided it was best to keep going. I'd drive slowly and carefully. If I got stopped I'd say my papers had been stolen. I had money. Something might turn up.

I got to Bordighera. I'd got through Ventimiglia all right. Going through Bordighera, I saw a restaurant. I'd had nothing since breakfast. So I went in. I thought I was safe enough by then.

I had finished eating and sat there relaxing, wondering what to do. The name 'Cassino' was on my mind. Where Maria had come from. There was something about it that was familiar, but I couldn't think what it was. I wondered if I was getting it mixed up with the casino at Monte Carlo.

A carabiniere came along the street. I saw him cross and come straight to the Buick. He walked all round it. He looked inside. He stood off and looked at it from the front. He went round and looked at it from the back. Then he looked at the restaurant, made up his mind, and came in. He came straight to me. I was the only customer.

'Scusi, signorina,' he said in Italian, 'but is that your Buick out there?'

I looked at him with what I hoped was a blank stare, as if I didn't understand, and asked him in French if he could speak French.

It was his turn to look blank. I thought that was lovely. It would be the end of it. I didn't see he had any real complaint about the car. It was parked reasonably enough. I thought it was time I got out of there. I picked up my camera and purse and went to stand up.

'Do you speak English?' he asked in English. He had an American accent.

Well, that was different. I had another look at him and decided he looked friendly. He was about thirty or so, so I took a gamble.

'Yes, I do,' I said. 'As a matter of fact, I am English. Or Scottish, rather. Why? What's the trouble, Officer?' I knew they liked being called Officer. He did. His face lit up. He pushed his cap up off his forehead.

'Waal now! What d'you know? Scottish, eh? Now ain't that somep'n? But say! How come you're drivin' a Buick? That's American. You get it in the States? You bin to the States? What, are you a tourist or somep'n?'

I told him I was. I'd just come from France. I'd got the Buick there. I was having a look round.

He was friendly. He'd only come to talk about the Buick. He'd thought I might have been American. His folks had moved there when he was small. They lived in Detroit where he'd gone to school and grown up. But he hadn't liked it. He'd come back to Italy and joined the Carabinieri. He was married and had twin boys aged six. Their godparents had sent them a model motor car each for their birthday. They were the same model Buicks as mine. That's what had caught his eye.

But it was his mention of godparents that did it for me. It jogged my mind about Cassino. My own godmother lived somewhere near there. If she were still alive and if I could find her, she might be able to help me.

I ordered coffee for us both and let him talk. He had himself a picnic. But I didn't mind. I felt gorgeously safe. He had steam he'd been building up for years. When he ran down, I asked him about Cassino. Where it was, how long it would take me to get there, how to find it? I told him I was going to visit my own godmother, the Countess of Vissochi. That impressed him as I'd hoped it would. He gave me everything he knew. And he gave me his name and where he was stationed. He said if I had any trouble to get in touch. That policeman was like a ray of sunshine to me.

It was late by the time I reached La Spezia, so I took his advice and stayed the night. I got to Roma for the second night. It was a long hard drive, but time was vital for me. At Viareggio, I turned off the coast road and went through Massarosa. He'd said it was shorter. From Roma I reached Cassino late on the third morning. I had no trouble locating the Countess. She was well known.

The house was similar to Bonne-maman's, but smaller and with smaller grounds. The maid said the Countess was in and would see me.

She looked every inch a Countess. She was small and old but very straight and dignified. She couldn't place me at first. I had to remind her of the dinner set with her crest on it, and about the trouble at Mother's wedding. I told her about Scotland.

'Oh yes,' she said. 'Of course. That was Beatrice, wasn't it? Yes, I remember. Oh, that was such a pity. He was a motor mechanic or something, wasn't he? Yes. Well, well. How the years do fly. And you're her daughter? And how is she?'

She wanted to know what I was doing in Italy. I told her I was having a look round. I was looking for a job and wanted to get across to France but didn't have a passport. Could she help? She said she thought she could. She asked if I had any money. I told her I had.

'Good,' she said. 'Then I think it can be arranged. We'll have to take you into Cassino and get you some Italian-made clothes and an Italian-style hairdo first. You'll never pass as you are. They'd know in a moment. You're unmistakably French. But I think we can do it.'

I stayed with her, and we did what she said. I was surprised at the difference it made. They accepted me as if I was one of them. The passport came through ten days later.

I got away early next morning. It had to be faced, and the sooner I faced it and got it done, the better. I had to get out of Italy. I hadn't had a good night's sleep since I'd been there. I'd no sooner get off than I'd be nightmare-ing. Every night it was the same. I'd be at the border post, and they'd tell me to come in. I'd go in, and there'd be another room off it. They'd put me in there. Then he'd come in. He was black and hairy and filthy. It would be awful. I'd hear them out in the other room, laughing. I'd wake up and be soaked in perspiration. I'm sure I'd been screaming. It was horrible facing people at breakfast.

I made better time. I didn't have to be so careful now that I had my passport. After Roma, I took the coast road. She'd said it was better and I'd see more. I wasn't interested in seeing anything. I only wanted to get back to France. I knew what could happen as long as I was in Italy.

I pushed on and made Grosseto for the first night, and Genova for the second. I wanted to get as close to the border as I could. I thought if I crossed in the morning there might be a different shift on. I'd thought of detouring at Savona and going through Cuneo and crossing through the Mt Clapier tunnel, but I'd lose too much time. I had to go through Ventimiglia.

Going through Bordighera, I called on the friendly policeman. I thought it was a good idea to refresh myself in his memory, just in case. I was very careful from then on until I got through Ventimiglia. I went like mad to get past their place and got to the border with no trouble. But there it happened just as it had in my dreams.

They asked me to please step inside. I had to. I couldn't do anything else. They took my passport and looked at it and at me. I could see the other door. They asked me questions. What was I going to France for? Did I have anything to declare? One of them went out and looked in the car. I told them I was going to see my sister in Paris. They gave me my passport and said I could go.

I must have looked awful silly. They had to tell me twice.

*   *   *

CHAPTER 19

Algeria

B ACK AT THE flat, there was a letter from Marie-Louise with another reply to my ad. They'd been there a fortnight. There'd been no changes at 241. Everything was all right. The reply was from Oran in Algeria, just across the Mediterranean from Marseille. It had a sort of personal challenge, and the writing had character. It was on ordinary paper and in English.

> Dear Miss or Madam, as the case may be; if you do indeed have the talents and fondness claimed in your advertisement in the *London Times*, and if you have not already found suitable employment for those talents, I can offer you work which, I do assure you, will not leave you cast off and unwanted after three years; work which will use and develop those talents to the utmost for as long as you wish, and the rewards will be great. Should you need assistance in finding me the Oran Police will readily give it to you. Aquinas of Ballineen.

I stewed on it for a couple of days. By its date, it was already three weeks old. He'd likely have someone by now. And it meant going farther away. I wanted to get back. I couldn't risk another Italy. I hadn't the time. On the other hand, I had nothing else. I didn't think there'd be any more replies. And if I went home to see how things were, there wouldn't be time to come back. I read it for the umpteenth time and decided I'd have to go and have a look.

In Marseille I found there was a ship going to Oran within three hours. I was on it. I left the Buick with the shipping agents. They'd send it on, freight collect, if I wanted it.

Oran was even hotter than I'd expected. The sun was pitiless. Aquinas was well known to the police. One of them took me to the native quartier. There were two boys about ten and twelve selling dates and homemade mats and baskets. He spoke to them in their own language. He told me they were from Ballineen and would take me there. He assured me I'd be quite safe with them. They looked like little monks with their bright, shining faces and long white robes. They had a small donkey.

They took me out along a dusty road that shimmered in the heat and seemed to lead to nowhere. A signpost said, 'To Sig and Sidi-bel-Abbes'. It was hard going in high heels. I thought of going barefoot as they were but knew my feet wouldn't stand it. They made room for me on the donkey, and then we made better time. I wondered what on earth had made me come.

We came to a collection of small buildings set around a courtyard. Over the entrance, it said 'Ballineen'. Other boys in ankle-length white robes came out.

As I got off the donkey, a man came out from one of the buildings. I knew instantly he must be Aquinas. He was dynamic. He was tall and lean and walked very straight. He moved with a lithe, easy swing. His head was tonsured, and he had a bright red bushy beard. He was dressed like the boys except that his robe was dark green. A heavy cross swung low from his waist. He had biblical sandals with thick motor-tyre soles. He came and took my hands in his and looked at me.

'So you came!' he said. He was about thirty. His eyes searched my face. They were green and deep set over broad, high cheekbones. His hands tightened and gave mine a little shake. 'How we prayed you would!' It came from his heart.

I didn't say anything. I guess I was too overwhelmed. I'd never seen anyone like him.

'You'd be the teacher of languages, wouldn't you now? From France?'

I nodded. I was thrilled by his deep voice and his beautiful brogue. He lifted his head and raised his eyes to heaven.

'Blessed be the name of the Lord,' he said fervently. 'For He shall hear thy prayers!' He let go one of my hands and put an arm along my shoulders. "Come then, Sister," he said. "Let us go in out of the sun and rest you. You must be weary."

He saw the camera hanging from my shoulder.

'But stay a moment,' he said. 'Do you have any film in that camera?'

I told him I had.

"Then show me how to work it and let us have a record of this blessed moment."

While I showed him, he said something to the boys, and they began chanting. The words were foreign to me, but the melody sounded like 'Danny Boy'. He said it was the 'Welcoming Song', sung for all new arrivals.

I told him I wasn't tired. I'd like to have a look round. He took me and showed me.

It was a home for unwanted native boys. There was room for 120. He ran it himself with public donations and by selling dates and small artefacts the boys made. He was a brother of a religious order based in Ireland, but he'd got into trouble dabbling in the politics and had to get out while he could. Ballineen was where he'd come from in County Cork. The boys ranged in age from four to sixteen. Some had come from the Courts, some had wandered in, and some he'd found himself. They were all well behaved and clean. The Oran Police helped him. They would overlook some minor offences if the offenders made a reasonable donation to Ballineen. The whole place was spotlessly neat and tidy. He had native women as house mothers but needed someone for the teaching. He was sure I was just what was wanted.

But I couldn't. It was good work, all right, but it wasn't for me. It was too harsh and pitiless. I wouldn't last anytime. I wasn't dedicated. Neither was I running away from anything. I was looking for what I'd been used to: a job as governess with a decent family. I was used to certain comforts. Had it been in kinder surroundings, I could have settled for it. I'd have done it for him. He'd have been marvellous to

ANNE ANGELO

work with. But not as it was. I'd soon dry out and be like the native women. I didn't want to leave my bones whitening in the sand.

Nothing would last there very long. Even in the shade, it was stifling. But out in the full glare, going from building to building, it was frightening. You had to run to get away from it.

And the flies were incredible. There was nothing they wouldn't do. You didn't get a moment's peace. Fifty or sixty would be clinging to your back, and a few peeled off, working on you. They'd fly into your mouth while you were speaking, settle on your open eyes, settle on your lips and crawl up inside your nose, fly right into your ears and set up a

At Aquinas's Home for boys 'Ballineen' near Sidi-bel-Abbes out of Oran.

Mad buzzing trying to get out again. When they got tired, others would take over. It was as if they were determined to make you submit. There was a crust of them round the donkey's eyes. They were disgusting.

I did think of staying on account of him.

He was one in a million. I'd never meet another like him. Inside all that saintliness, there was a normal, strong, healthy man, and he had no one.

I told him I was very sorry, but I couldn't do it. It was good work, and it was a credit to him, but it wasn't what I was used to. I wouldn't be able to stand the heat. I didn't have his endurance. I felt I was slapping him and his God in the face. He'd pinned so much on me.

He took it marvellously. He said he quite understood. I didn't have anything to be sorry for. I'd done nothing wrong. It was harsh. He knew it was. He'd send me back in the morning when the boys went in to market. The women would fix me something for the night.

But he was so dynamic I was afraid if I stayed one night, it would lead to another, and I'd never get away. I told him I'd like to go immediately if I could. There might be a ship going, and if there was, I'd like to be on it. Time was important. I said if he could lend me some sandals or something, I'd walk it. I'd leave them with the police for him. It would be getting cooler; it wouldn't be so bad.

But he wouldn't hear of it. He got me a camel. He said it would be quicker and more comfortable. He sent a boy with me to bring it back.

When it came to going, I nearly didn't. He was so terrific. If the die hadn't been cast, I wouldn't have gone.

He'd just put me up; the camel was still on its knees. All the boys were standing round watching.

'Before you go', he said, my hands firmly in his, 'I want you to promise me something. I want you to promise that if you ever have nowhere to go and need a roof over your head, you'll come back here. You won't have to stay. You can make it your home until you find something. It doesn't matter when it is nor how far away you are, you'll always be welcome. If you need money to get here, let me know. I'll help if I can. Now promise you will.'

He made me ashamed of myself. I wondered if there was any chance he was feeling the same way about me that I was about him. But I decided not. He'd be like it with anybody. So I promised. He blessed me and put the boy up and let us go. I didn't look back. I daren't. I knew he'd still be standing there.

I'd never ridden a camel before, but once I got used to the motion, it was good. We got along fine. I felt like one of the wise men from the East. But I had to pay for it. The assortment of ticks and lice I got from it gave me the devil of a time.

There wasn't a ship to Marseille for two days, so I went to the police to get the name of a good hotel. They gave me one and also told me the Italian Consul was in Oran. They thought he might be able to help me. They rang and made an appointment for me for the next day. He was only going to be there for the one day.

At the hotel, I met Olga Morrison. She'd arrived from Casablanca that morning to rejoin her husband in Marseille. He was the British representative for Massey-Harris, the machinery people. She was White Russian, he was English. She was the only other English-speaking person at the hotel, and we spent most of our time together. We crossed in the same ship.

I met the Consul, and he was very helpful. He knew my godmother, the Countess. He said he'd do anything he could for me. If he heard of anything, he'd let me know. We had coffee at a small roadside cafe. I got the waiter to take a photograph. I thought I'd send a copy to the Countess. But I never did.

*   *   *

At the roadside cafe in Oran having coffee with the Italian Consul.

CHAPTER 20

Return To Lille

O LGA'S HUSBAND WAS waiting for her in Marseille. They were going to Paris, making stops at Bordeaux, Poitiers, and other places. They wanted that we should go together in convoy, and it could have been fun if I hadn't been under pressure of time. He was nice but very old-school-tie. I wanted to go to Bordeaux. The Countess had given me addresses of my mother's people there and at Mont-de Marsan and Perigueux. She'd said I ought to call on them. They'd be pleased to see me. But I didn't want to be in a hurry. I wanted to be able to stay a few days. And I didn't want to go as a country cousin needing help. I wanted to be a success, maybe with my own family. Anyway, I had to go back to Monaco for the things I'd left at the flat. So I left the Morrisons in Marseille and didn't run into them again until the war.

It looked as if the worst had happened when I got to 241. It took me four more days. I stayed the night at the flat and got away first thing in the morning. Which meant I'd been away for thirty-five days. I drove in round the back and up to the patio steps. There was nobody anywhere. The garden was neglected. Everything seemed deserted. I Yoo-hoo-ed going up and in but got no answer. It wasn't until I got up into my own rooms that I found anybody. Marie-Louise was there packing my things. We both had a good cry. She was quite sure she'd never see me again. It'd been over a month since my letter. There were only nine days left. She was going to send everything to Invergordon for me. She was more worried than I was. She had the two Jacques to think of. I only had myself.

There'd been no movement with the house. Plenty had come and looked, and all had said it was nice but too big. Bonne-maman had been a few times, but she'd had nothing definite either. Nobody could settle to work. It was like waiting for a sentence to be passed. It was awful. There wasn't time to advertise again. I had nowhere to go and didn't know what I was going to do. I couldn't even settle to my packing although I knew it would have to be done.

There was so much of it, and I hadn't half enough suitcases and trunks. And if I did get it packed, I didn't know what I was going to do with it. It would cost me a fortune to take it home, and I didn't know if Father would let me in when I got there. And anyway, it'd be no good to me there. I'd never be able to wear any of it. They'd think I was mad. I'd freeze. That whole huge wardrobe was packed tight—dresses, frocks, costumes, and coats. All the drawers were full. A row of shoes filled in the full length of the back wall. There were eighteen parasols hanging on the rails along the insides of the doors. It was all good stuff. A lot of it Bonne-maman had given me. I just couldn't leave it for someone else to paw through. Although I did think of that. I thought of leaving everything and going back to Ballineen, but I knew I couldn't. In the mornings, I'd start to make two piles. One to take and one to leave. But by the end of the day, I'd be no further ahead and put it all away again and shut the doors.

It got down until we only had five days left. It was well after lunch. We were all in the butler's pantry—Marie-Louise, Heloise, old Jacques, and me. Young Jacques was off somewhere after a job. We weren't talking. We were just sitting there having the gloomies. The dirty dishes were still on the table. The door opened, and in came Bonne-maman. She wasn't happy.

'So!' she said, leaning with both hands on the top of her walking stick and looking from one to the other of us. 'This is what you do all day, is it? No wonder the place is in a mess. I've been all over it looking for you. I thought you'd all gone. Marie-Louise! You're in charge here. Why isn't the work being done? You're all still getting paid, aren't you? Well then, what's the trouble? What do you think your master would say if he came and saw it? Well? Aren't any of you going to answer me?'

I tried to explain how difficult it was. With only a skeleton staff, it wasn't possible to keep it like it used to be. And with only five days left, there seemed no sense in trying. Everything was so hopeless.

'Nothing's hopeless at all,' she snapped. 'How do any of you know what the future holds? But that's not the point. They're still being paid, and they should still be doing the work. I'm not talking about you, my dear. I know you've been doing your best. I've seen your advertisements. By the way, how did you get on at Monte Carlo? Did you have any success?'

'No. I didn't. Why? How did you know about that?'

'I had a letter from the concierge at the flats. He wondered if you had my authority. Did you have to wait for someone, did you?'

I started to tell her about it, but she stopped me.

'Not just for a moment, my dear. I want to have a talk with you, but let me get these people away first. Come on, then, off you go. There's plenty of the day left yet. Jacques! You can get onto those lawns. And when you've done all them, you can get into the flowerbeds. Heloise! You take your dusters and get into the salons. You'll find, in the main one, where I've written in the dust on the grand piano. And when you've finished there, you'll find plenty up the main staircase. Marie-Louise! Get this pantry tidied up, please, will you? I want to have a talk with Anne here. And there's no need for any of you to think it's hopeless. You never know what might turn up.'

When Jacques and Heloise had gone, she pulled out a chair and sat down, and we talked about what I'd been doing. I told her it was too late to advertise again, and I still had nowhere to go.

She waited until Marie-Louise had gone and the door was shut, and then she asked me if I had any money. I told her I had. I hadn't got much, but I had a bit.

'Yes,' she said, with a little twinkle in her eye. 'I rather fancy you have. You're a good manager, aren't you? You don't waste anything. I think you've probably done very well since you came to us. Well now. How would you like to stay on here? I think you could, you know. You could stay on and run this place as a kind of guesthouse or private hotel.

It would be better for him to have it occupied than having it shut up. What do you say to that for an idea?'

It was a fantastic idea. But I couldn't see it had any sense, for me. My little bit wouldn't last long trying to run a place as big as that. There'd be staff and food. The rent alone would soon clean me out. Besides, I'd never done anything like that. I wouldn't know how to start.

'No. Of course you wouldn't,' she said. 'And you'll never learn, will you, until you try? You've got good connections. You've just been telling me about your people in the South and your godmother the Countess. I didn't know you had a background like that. It's probably why you mix so well. People recognise that sort of thing. You could cater to the better class of guest. I might be able to send you people. And I'm sure he could. You might have to run at a loss for a couple of months, but you could manage that, couldn't you? I think most of the staff would come back. Marie-Louise would know about that. She'd probably know where to find most of them. Let her handle the staff while you look after the guests and the management. I think you could do it.'

It sounded a marvellous idea. If only I could do it. But I didn't see how I could. It was too big. I didn't have enough. There'd be the wages and the food. There'd be the rent, and I'd have to advertise. I told her I didn't have enough. I'd lose everything.

'Yes', she said, 'it is a gamble. But I think it will pay off. It will all depend on when you get your first guests. And how you treat them. The best advertising, my dear, you know is by word of mouth. You treat people right, and they'll tell their friends. And you wouldn't need all the staff to begin with. Just enough to get the place cleaned up again. As things move, you can get the others. I might be able to get him to reduce the rent for you. I'd have spoken to him about it before, but there was no sense until I knew what your plans were. Now what do you say? Shall I try?'

I didn't know what to say. The size and cheek of it took my breath away. I'd never have dreamed of it, but she made it sound so possible.

'Look at it from his point of view,' she said. 'For three months, he's tried to sell it or let it, and he's done no good. They all say it's too big. Well, all right, so it's too big. He can't alter that. And he can't alter the way things are going in Germany either. He can keep on paying wages if he wants to, but there's no sense in it. He can do it indefinitely and get nowhere. He knows it's going to pieces. It'll be worse if he shuts it up. The vandals will get into it. They'll wreck it completely. As likely as not, they'll set it on fire. He doesn't want that. It'd be better for him to have someone living in it. Someone he knows and can trust. You're the most likely person, my dear. Marie-Louise hasn't got the ability. I think he'd be very pleased if he knew you were interested. Well? Will you give it a try?'

I got up and went round behind her and hugged her. I felt I had to do something, and it seemed the most natural. It was a thing I'd often wanted to do. I pressed a kiss into her hair and told her if she could do this for me, I'd be grateful for the rest of my life. And she liked it, although she made out she didn't.

'Now, now', she murmured, gently freeing herself, 'there's no need for any of that, my dear. It's as much for him as it is for you. And you deserve it. You've been a good girl and never let us down. All right, then, I'll see what I can do. But I wouldn't mention it to the others, though. Just in case things go wrong.'

And I didn't. Although they kept asking me about my packing— when was I going to get on with it?

It was Thursday afternoon. We had to be out by the Friday. She rang and said it was all settled. The rent would be a nominal one franc a month. I could have it as long as things continued as they were and as long as I looked after the furniture and kept the place in good repair. It could be terminated by six months' notice in writing by either of us. He wished me good luck with it and said he'd send me people if he could.

That was a heady moment. I had the maddest urge to rush round and do crazy things. But I knew I couldn't. Not anymore. Things would have to be different. I think that was when I really grew up. It was like when I'd first walked down those stairs in my new French clothes. I'd put aside everything Scottish and become a new person. Here it was again. I'd put off being a governess and become the mistress. The

ANNE ANGELO

whole house was mine to do as I liked with. They were my staff. It was a marvellous feeling.

I went and told them. When they all said they'd stay on with me, I got some champagne for them. I thought it was a day to celebrate.

*   *   *

CHAPTER 21

The Threat Approaches

I T WAS A marvellous success right from the start. I was amazed by how easy it was. Everything fell into place as if it had all been there just waiting for me.

The first thing I did was to shift into M'sieu's bureau. It was the master suite. And from it I'd be better able to know what was going on. The small landing where its few steps met the main staircase let me see down into the foyer and out through the portico down to the footpath. The windows at the rear gave me a clear view over the whole garden to the back gates. And the rooms were better. The bathroom was the best in the house. It was a dream. Not only were the tiles and colour scheme better, but the towel rails were actually chromed hot-water pipes so the towels were always warm and snuggly. There were polished-copper hot-water pipes in the cupboards to keep pyjamas and things heavenly to get into.

It took Heloise and me a full day to do the shifting. It was then I found out how much stuff I had. I'd never have got it all packed. She thought it was silly, me having so much. She thought my parasols were especially crazy.

'But, madame', she said, 'what's the good of them? You can't use them. They'd think you were silly going out with a parasol these days. I don't believe in keeping a lot of junk.'

But they weren't junk. Not to me. Apart from being the most exquisitely feminine things I had, each one was a memento. A souvenir of some place I'd been. Mostly with Bonne-maman. Each one had a story. They represented steps in my development. I hung them along the rail on my wardrobe doors in the order I'd got them, and they looked lovely.

Then Marie-Louise got me the staff I wanted. I didn't get them all. Only enough to get the place all cleaned up again. Bonne-maman gave us a month and then came and looked us over. She was pleased.

'Yes, my dear,' she said as we came back down the main staircase. 'That's more like it. I knew you could do it. That's much better than the way it was going. He'll be very pleased. Well now, I suppose you're nearly ready for some guests, aren't you? Have you had any response to your advertisements yet?'

I hadn't, and I told her so. She didn't mention it again. But a fortnight later, I had a phone call from Paris asking if I could accommodate a family of four overnight in three days' time. Could I? It sent everybody scurrying like beavers to get ready in time.

I got the rest of the staff. I didn't take Albert the butler. He was a good one and everybody knew him, but he couldn't see there'd been a change. I was no longer the children's governess to be treated with scorn and condescension. And that was a pity, because I'd had all I wanted of that. So I got a new one. A six-foot ex-army sergeant major named Alphonse. He was most impressive. I kept old Jacques on as an undergardener and young Jacques as odd jobs. I did that for Marie-Louise, although she didn't ask me to. I wanted her to be happy. And it was a good thing I did. The three of them saved my bacon lots of times when the war came.

Those first guests turned out to be the Villeneuves from Morez in the Franche-Comté. We'd called on them when we got back into France after taking the shortcut up the mountain zigzag coming home from the Winter Sports in Lausanne. There were the four of them, the parents and two grown-up daughters. They were holidaying going through to Norway and Sweden. When I found out that Bonne-maman had written them about me and 241, I set out to make their stay as enjoyable as I could. And I must've succeeded. They booked for one night and stayed a week.

The girls were eighteen and twenty-one and about as romantic as I'd been when I first came to Lille. So I put them in my Louis XIV. I thought it would appeal to them. And it did. They were in ecstasies over it. I put the parents in the Gold Room next door, and they thought it was perfect. They spent hours out on the balcony looking down over the traffic in the Rue Nationale.

The weather was good, so I took them out everywhere I could think of. I tried to show them things they wouldn't see at home. I drove them out to Neuville-en-Ferrain to have a look at the Maginot Line. I took them to the Citadelle. It's a huge massive fortress built in the 1670s by Vauban and Simon Vollant. It's still regarded as one of the great marvels of military architecture. I packed an al fresco lunch so we could make a day of it.

I took them and showed them how Lille got its name where the Basilique Notre Dame de la Treille now stands. In the tenth century, the Comtes de Flandre built an important chateau there. It was then an island in the Basse-Deule. It's from that island—l'ile—that the name 'Lille' was formed. The Basilique was begun in 1854. Our oldest building, though, is the Chapelle Notre Dame de Reconciliation. It was built in the thirteenth century. I took them to so many churches and places and told them so much about them that they were quite convinced Lille was my hometown. I didn't see any reason to tell them otherwise. But it did show me how completely French I'd become.

I filled their evenings by taking them to the opera, the ballet, and the theatre. They were all musical. The girls could play quite well. So I arranged musical evenings. I had a full grand piano in the main salon and a boudoir grand in the small one. The girls played for me and the staff in the small salon. And I brought in singers and musicians so they could play in concert with professionals in the big salon. And they were well able to hold their own. The parents were as proud as punch. When it came time to go, they all said they'd never had such an enjoyable stay. They'd come again for their next holidays. And they'd certainly tell their friends about me. And that was all I wanted. It'd been hectic, and I was considerably out of pocket, but it turned out a good investment.

From then on, the world beat a path to my doors. And it was the sort of world I wanted. Wealthy people, influential people, society figures—they came from all over France. I had government ministers and members of the House of Representatives; prominent people in the arts, the opera and the ballet; notables from show business and radio. I made sure the society columnists knew what was going on at 241 Rue Nationale. The parties in my dining room and salons, the brilliant crowds of elegant people chatting over their champagne in my foyer became news. I'd arrived.

And I learned about tact and discretion and the odd little quirks people had. For instance, one very high official in the Department of Finance came with his wife so often that we became good friends. He would quietly drop me the hint that this country or that country was about to de-value or re-value its currency. In the strictest confidence, of course. I was able to do very well for myself. On the other hand, this same gentleman had a thing against flowers. I had flowers everywhere. Particularly at the foot of the main staircase in front of the big mirror. Poor Alphonse my butler would come to me in great distress. 'Madame! Please! You really must speak to him. He is impossible. Come and see. And they are only freshly arranged.'

And there, heaped on the heart of a rose or filling the trumpet of a lily or hibiscus would be a pile of cigar ash. And I had plenty of ashtrays everywhere. He took a delight in it. But what could I do? Could I go and remonstrate with him when he'd just put me in the way of making enough to buy every flower in the market ten times over? And how could I explain to Alphonse why I couldn't? I had to just get fresh flowers and let Alphonse think what he liked. I know I lost face in his eyes.

Some of the men gave me problems in other ways too. Ways that didn't endear them to me in the least. I suppose I was an attractive proposition to them. I was on my own and obviously doing very well. But some of them had their wives with them. I wasn't interested in any affairs like that. If they'd do that to their wives, what would they do to me when they met someone new and my time was finished? I was looking for someone, yes, of course I was. If an Aquinas or someone like my brother Peter had come along, my life would have been complete. It was hard work on my own. But I'd find him someday. In the meantime,

I was making good hay and wanted to keep on doing it while I could. I was well aware that, that 'can be terminated by six months' notice in writing' could be applied at any time. I wanted to get as much behind me as I could.

It was about this time, as I mingled and I thought on more than an even footing with these people, that I began to wonder how it had all come about. How it was me here doing this.

When I first came to this house, I must have been as gauche as gauche. How proud I'd been of myself in my Bonnie Prince Charlie costume. I wondered what they'd really thought of me. I still had it, Glengarry and all, carefully packed away in Mother's suitcase at the back of my wardrobe. How had it come about that I was now the elegant cosmopolitan running this fashionable hotel? And elegant cosmopolitan I had to be, or else they'd never have accepted me on equal terms.

In those six weeks when we'd been cleaning up and getting organised, I'd had time on my hands in the evenings, and I'd re-read Shakespeare. M'sieu'd left most of his books in the bureau. We'd had Shakespeare at home. Mother had got him for us. She'd said there was great wisdom in his writings. And there was too. But some of it wasn't. There was one thing in particular that stuck in my mind. I'd come across it again. In his Julius Caesar, he makes Cassius tell Brutus, 'The fault, Dear Brutus, is not in our stars but in ourselves that we are underlings.' It's just not true.

What we are is due almost entirely to our stars. I don't mean that I'm a great believer in horoscope or anything like that. By stars I mean the parents we're born to, the place and time we're born in, and the circumstances we're born into; the lives our parents lived before they married; the people we meet in our formative years; yes, and afterwards too.

I hadn't got this hotel because of any marvellous ability in me. Not at all. Any of the others—Marie-Louise, Charlotte, or Heloise—would have made out just as well. It wasn't luck either. It's luck when you put money on a number at roulette and it wins. This hadn't been like that. It'd been due to things that had happened before. Mostly through Bonne-maman.

ANNE ANGELO

If I hadn't stood up to her that first day we met and threatened to get the police, she'd never have taken me under her wing. I'd have gone the way of all the others. I could have been as good as good, and it wouldn't have mattered. Lots of people spend their entire lives as perfect angels of goodness but never get anywhere. Because there's no one standing by to notice and give them a push. And I wouldn't have fought back like that if I hadn't been taught to as a child. It probably came from Father because he'd had a rough time when he was a child.

And even having her there, pushing for me, wouldn't have been any good if I hadn't had the money in the bank. And I wouldn't have had that but for Father. Peter and I'd had to learn about money the hard way, by selling our flowers and whisky to the sailors at the naval base.

She'd said that my ability to mix with people had probably come from my mother. And I think she was right. These were my mother's people. This was the sort of world she'd been brought up in. The sort of world I'd have been born into if Father hadn't taken her away to Scotland. It was as if a wheel had turned full circle, bringing me back. I wondered what for. I wanted to go to Bordeaux, Perigueux, and Mont-de-Marsan to see what would come of it, but I was too busy and kept putting it off. Things were a bit uncertain with Germany, and I wanted to keep making my hay while my sun was shining.

We had three bad scares. One was in June 1938, one in September the same year, and one in June 1939. Each time, my guests fled, and I was left with an empty house. On the last one, in June 1939, I followed them. I packed what I could into the Oldsmobile and fled to Paris. At that time, I had the original Buick, a 1937 Buick and a new Olds I'd got from America through Cherbourg. Alphonse looked after the cars. He was good. He'd been in Transport in the army. I felt so foolish when nothing happened and I had to come back to 241 that I didn't do that again although there was always the worry.

For a long time, I'd been wanting to go home to see my mother. Her health worried me. I also wanted to see how Father was towards me. I'd had no word from him. It seemed to me that if things got much worse with Germany, I might be wise to get out. And the only place I had was Scotland. But it would depend on him. Whether he'd let me or not.

So when we heard on 20 August that Germany and Russia had signed a Non-Aggression Pact, I decided to go. I'd go for a fortnight. If things were all right, I'd send for the rest of my things and stay. The house was going smoothly. Alphonse could look after the guests, and Marie-Louise could handle the rest. I left on the twenty-sixth. But it was a mistake. I should never have done it. Things were never the same afterwards. But maybe it wasn't a mistake: it was just something I had to do.

*   *   *

ANNE ANGELO

9781669888376